1

UNITY CENTER
OF EDMONTON
477-5351

LIGHT FOR OUR AGE

By Robert P. Sikking

UNITY BOOKS•UNITY VILLAGE, MO.

CONTENTS

CHAPTER I

As historians endeavor to sort out the mid-twentieth century, there will be a number of unique peculiarities that will vie for the recognition that will help to set this era apart from others. The middle of the twentieth century marked the birth of the nuclear age. It marked the first exciting steps that man would take toward conquest of space.

In this period, specifically following World War II with its bestial inhumanity expressed by man toward man, there has been the birth of social conscience as never before expressed. Never before in the history of man have so many human beings been so concerned about the well-being of so many others. Oddly enough, coexisting with this brotherly concern there has erupted once again a breakdown of individual moral and ethical standards. That breakdown has produced forms of personal violence and isolation that manifest in loneliness and separation to a staggering degree in the very midst of the greatest concentration of urbanized living in history.

During this period, greater strides have been taken in mass communication than were taken throughout all the rest of preceding history. Just in one generation, from parent to child (and even more so between grandparent and grandchild), the increase in communication has expanded awareness to such a degree that we have coined a phrase that requires no elucidation in our time: "the generation gap." Whereas in the early decades of this century the family unit had a cohesiveness, we see an increasing deterioration of the significance of family in the mid-twentieth century. Surely this has been abetted by "the generation gap" to a very marked degree.

It would appear that this era heralds also either the beginning of the end of formal religious "churchianity," or a transitional period that will bring about a whole new ecclesiastical experience for man. At the beginning of the twentieth century, throughout Europe and the Americas as well as elsewhere in the world, there was an extremely high proportion of those whose lives revolved around "the church." There has been a staggering change in this area of our social experience. Fifty to a hundred years ago, conformity was the norm in Judeo-Christian experience; the mid-century has brought about the development of a spiritual "do-it-yourself" trend that may spell doom for organized religious experience as we have known it in the past few centuries. It may well herald also the advent of a spiritual maturity that can change man more than all his technical and scientific advances will.

Our vocabulary during this time has changed rapidly. In addition to the new words and phrases that are born of the advances of scientific and technological understanding, our value judgments have given greater significance to words and phrases that may typify this era in history. As never before, we have become "environmentalists," ever conscious of "pollution." Ecology has become so popular that even youngsters are able to understand and communicate effectively within its perimeters. "Anti-pollution" has become a positive thrust of this time. Anti-pollution drives seek to cleanse our atmosphere, our water sources, our earth, and our exposure one to another. We have developed anti-pollution laws, devices, and slogans.

The birth and rapid development of the science of cybernetics has had a most dramatic effect upon our way of life in this period of our history. The word *cybernetics* was introduced and the field popularized in a book published in 1948 by the mathematician Norbert Wierner. Automation, data-processing, and computerization through the science of cybernetics have produced what historians may well term "the second Industrial Revolution." Not only have we freed, to a staggering degree, the muscle of man; we have begun to free his brain as well.

Though perhaps yet undiscernable to most people, the mid-twentieth century is the period of history in which man shall be seen to have emerged into the infancy of his spiritual generation as a self-cognizant divine being. Those of us living through this period of time, though often pressed to the limit, are in reality living in the most exciting time of all. This is a time of awakening, when we still retain a remembrance of the past that has made possible the new day into which we are emerging. The infinite possibilities that lie before us are at the same time exciting, frightening, thrilling, and pregnant with hope. The renaissance through which we are passing at this time will necessitate a clarification by historians; there is a difference between that which occurred from the fourteenth to the sixteenth century and that which is occurring in the middle of the twentieth century. It is a renaissance nonetheless, because it is the rebirth in the consciousness of man of his divinity, his nobility, his inseparable oneness with the infinity of God.

History, if it can be called a science, is at best an inaccurate one. One can read conscientious historical volumes on a period of history during which he has lived in his adult life. He can compare them with his own recollections, and invariably discrepancies appear. If we don't get too close to the details or the "nitty gritty" of any period in history, and thus avoid creating a credibility gap, there is an overview that can be educational to us in our ongoing evolution as divine creatures.

Tracing the history of spiritual evolution back through time, we can draw some logical conclusions that will enable us to find a beginning point from which to progress and have a better perspective of where we are spiritually and where we are going from that point. The history of the Judeo-Christian tradition, to those who have evolved out of it, is reasonably accurate and therefore acceptable to us. Though there are tremendous gaps and inconsistencies in it, there is a sense of continuity that is reasonable to us. That reasonableness is supported by our innate feelings of belief, our faith. A tremendous part of the validity of our religious history is based upon our desire to believe its accuracy and truth.

Prior to but overlapping our Judeo-Christian era is that era which brought forth the Greco-Latin civilization. This period and its traditions had and still have a tremendous bearing on our own. Prior to the overlapping again was the ancient Egyptian civilization, which also had and still has a bearing on succeeding

8

civilizations and traditions. The Encyclopedia Brittanica estimates that the ancient Egyptian civilization existed for thousands of years and terminated sometime in the eighth century before Christ. The Greco-Latin civilization, with the tremendous advances of the Greeks and Romans, came into being prior to the demise of the Egyptian civilization and lasted to and beyond the earliest days of our own Judeo-Christian civilization, which brings us down into our own age in the middle of the twentieth century.

The study of history from the perspective of the evolution of religious thought and tradition is a vast, exciting, and illuminating one. The purpose of this work is not to consider all of the major historical eras that have brought mankind where he is today. Rather, our purpose is to touch on a few of those highlights which will show a thread of evolution that can give us additional insight by which we may proceed from where we are to attain all that lies ahead of us.

Prior to the ancient Egyptian civilization (from which we have some considerable volume of data, artifacts, and tradition), there were the eons of time through which man evolved, leaving so few traces that our search must rely on suppositions. There is evidence that makes it reasonable to suppose that man has always had a sense of, a belief in, and an awareness of deity. The number, forms, type, and purposes of deity have differed, but it is safe to assume that so long as man has been a self-conscious entity, he has also been conscious of deity. There is a correlation between self-consciousness and god-consciousness, as we shall see.

CHAPTER II

A favorite pastime of intellectual, god-oriented men has been to hypothesize about the religious, spiritual traditions of others. It is impossible to approach, stand beside, and touch the Stonehenge megaliths near Salisbury, in England, without imagining all sorts of things about the worship practices of the ancients. To climb the steps of the great pyramids, in Mexico or in Egypt, is to activate the yearnings of our soul to know more of how men have believed, prayed, and worshiped, so that credence may be given to our own methods and systems of belief.

It is safe to assume that men have always been motivated by some kind of belief in deity, no matter how naive. Perhaps in his earliest dawnings on this planet Earth, man's state could be compared to that of an infant or a small child. Not having developed an intellectual grasp of deity, man had much more of a sense of the nearness of deity, rather than in intellectual, communicable understanding. A child has a sense of reality that is not confused by intellectual awareness; thus we envy his childlike resilience and trust and faith. There is no question in the child's mind about the ability of the cow to jump over the moon. Perhaps he is infinitely wiser than we know before we succeed in polluting his consciousness with our beliefs in limitation of time, space, etc.

It is difficult to imagine that there was not a sense of adoration or even worship of the sources of his comfort, safety, or fulfillment. Is not the infant's love for the mother born of an instinctive realization that from her comes that which fulfills, feeds, sustains, and protects him? That men worshiped deity in the field, in trees and water around them, is accepted as reasonable. To this day, we have the carry-over of a belief that a god of fortune dwelt in trees—we still "knock on wood" when we seek the assurance of avoiding an undesirable experience. As man perceived that the great light of the day was a source of warmth (and nonintellectually sensed that it was the source of life), all civilizations in one way or another worshiped the sun. It only took a little reasoning (which we might mistakenly call superstition) to believe that the moon, or that which inhabited it, was also deity. Many centuries were to pass before we understood intellectually that the sun's rays do in fact function to produce life, and that the moon's invisible emanations affect our tides and more directly the observable cycles of our physical life.

Deity must have been, in those earliest dawnings, a reality that man experienced. Perhaps he did not understand (as we think of understanding) but he knew, he *sensed* deity, and dwelt in an interrelated coexistence with deity. To a child, his parents and what they represent in the way of security, sustenance, comfort, and fulfillment are not separate—they are a part of him even as his hands or feet are a part of him. A child coexists with the extension of himself that is the parental presence.

12

It was necessary for man to evolve his awareness of deity in order that he might consciously, as an act of will, demonstrate that deity. It is through this process that man moves from a state of bliss in coexistence with deity to an understanding awareness of himself as deity. As we shall see, we are in the process of evolving from unity with God to conscious, willed unity *as* God. At no point along the way have we been separate from God, nor have we erred or failed or sinned in the way that we have always believed. As we see ourselves in spiritual, historical perspective we will not only understand this apparent enigma, but we will see clearly the way that we shall proceed.

It is reasonable to assume that in the earliest phases of man's evolution, religion was creedless. Man had not yet evolved to a point where it was necessary for him to declare his belief to himself, let alone to others. It was not until the origins of the ancient Egyptian civilization, and on through the Greek and Roman civilizations, that man began to develop what we call anthropomorphic polytheism.

Often deity did not appear to have sustained, blessed, or answered the need of man, and it was logical that his concept of worship must include something that would engender favor in deity to dispose "it" to change "its" way toward man. Perhaps it was at this point in reasoning that man began to develop anthropomorphism—the "conception of god with human attributes."

Anthropomorphic polytheism—that is, the belief in more than one god in human form—came into being as a logical, sequential thought of man as reason began to develop in him. His belief in deity was still creedless, for it consisted simply of performing those rites or rituals that were believed to appease the deity in order to obtain a desired result. It was necessary to curry favor of the god or goddess of the harvest in order to assure a good crop. Man came to sacrifice to the god or goddess of fertility if he wished to be assured of a productive life in which he might multiply his kind. Fructification in one way or another was the purpose of almost all early worship.

The concept of duality—good and evil—came into being as a logical result of anthropomorphism. Since it was evident that the world was peopled with all sorts—kind and mean, gentle and rough, helpful and hurtful—it was not difficult to develop an awareness of "the good guys vs. the bad guys." It was only one step further to the development of good deities and destructive deities. To the Greeks of old, Artemis was the mother goddess, the very personification of chastity, whereas Ares was a god of violent death and destruction.

Choosing one's household god or goddess was perhaps one of the very early expressions of will as it expressed through theism—belief in deity. There are people in the world today who believe in more than one god, and their polytheism allows them the inherent right to choose the god or goddess they worship. Even as recently as the sixties, I watched the Christian observance of burial of an African which, under cover of darkness, was followed by disinterment so that pagan rites could be performed for the benefit of the deceased and those left behind.

It is difficult if not impossible to pin down accurately when mankind evolved from one state of consciousness into another. Sometime between four to eight centuries before Jesus Christ, the concept of

14

one God evolved in the Judaic civilization and tradition. The concept of one transcendent god was indeed one of the most significant advances in the evolution of mankind. It was an idea that did not catch on very rapidly, however. Toynbee makes reference to this point in mankind's evolution by pointing out that "divinity was drained out of nature and placed in one transcendent God." It was at that point, he suggests, that there occurred "the genesis of pollution."

Without any question, the pollution in man's thinking became evident at that point when he conceived of the one transcendent God. At that point, we were given the key to dominion. Perhaps it is true that we allowed divinity to be drained out of nature, and thus began a long period of disrespect for our environment. It was not that we had conceived of a transcendent God, but that we could not grasp the allness and onliness of that God.

The mistake we made was in putting our God away from us. Unable to define the nature of infinity with our finite consciousness, we found it necessary to relegate our new-found deity to another realm, another world. With this, we introduced into our faltering understanding the concept of "otherworldliness." Instead of allowing our God to be understood as omnipresence, omnipotence, and omniscience, we succeeded only in wrapping Him in "otherworldliness" and allowed Him to take on larger proportions, greater love, vaster power, and more encompassing wisdom than we could conceive for ourself.

We placed our God "up there." We gave Him superhuman characteristics. We came to believe that His hand could smite us, His eyes could see us, His voice could be heard in the land. We defined His realm as having portals of pearl, streets of gold, and an administration conducted by sword-bearing super-angels.

In the infinite wisdom of God, the fact that we "failed" to perceive of the allness and onliness of God, the "mistake" that we made in putting our God away from us, was not and is not failure or mistake. Every step along the way of our soul's unfoldment has been in divine order. Now let us understand clearly what we are considering here. All through the eons of time that man has trodden the pathway of evolution, every seeming mistake, error, failing, or sin has been a part of divine order. It must then have all been a part of divine will!

Let us here do a little postulating. Either we live in and are an intrinsic part of a universe that is based upon principle, or we live in and are part of happenstance . . . chance. You see, it must be the one or the other, for the two cannot coexist. Either there is principle, or there isn't. It certainly seems reasonable to assume that if it can be proved that there is a single principle, then there has to be some other explanation for what appears to be happenstance. All logical reasoning must be based upon a postulate that is accepted as true. We may be unable to prove our postulate, but there has to be a point where we accept, where we believe, where we start with faith.

The science of mathematics is based upon principle. There is no way in which the laws of mathematics can be disproved, for they are based upon a principle. *Two plus two equals four.* How simple the principle here shared! It is totally unreasonable to assume that under certain circumstances, two plus two might equal seven! Though a child might, in working the simple problem, come up with seven as the answer, that does not in any way alter the truth, the principle involved. Two plus two still does and always will equal four. It is inconceivable that the law of mathematics could coexist with chance in regard to its application.

The dictionary gives as one of the definitions of principle "a synonym for God." Let us then postulate that the concept of "otherworldliness" in relation to God, the one transcendent God, is totally inappropriate. Instead of being apart from us as a separate being, God is "closer . . . than breathing, nearer than hands and feet." This concept was not new when Tennyson first penned these lines in the nineteenth century. Earlier, Voltaire said, "If God is not in us, He never existed." In the first century Seneca, the Roman Stoic philosopher said, "Call it nature, fate, fortune; all these things are names of the one and selfsame God." Earlier still, Jesus Christ said, "I and my Father are one." In his search for identity, Moses is recorded as having inquired how he could define God to others. "God said to Moses, 'I AM WHO I AM.' And he said, 'Say this to the people of Israel, I AM has sent me to you.' "

CHAPTER III

"I AM WHO I AM." These simple words have been an enigma to man for centuries. He has reasoned that there must be a great mystical significance in them, and has meditated at length in hope that the enigma might be resolved. At the risk of oversimplufication let us alter the tempo, the emphasis we put on the words. In doing so, they may well give depth of insight to us. "I AM WHO I AM." Perhaps the infinite wisdom of our one transcendent God is saying to us that the "I AM" in you has arrived at some degree of self-awareness. Could it be that He is saying, "I am not something apart; I am that something in you that has perceived of identity"?

The mineral world has identity, but could be said not to have perceived of its identity. Iron or zinc or gold are what they are. There is an "intelligence" that permits (or even more, insists) that they conform to what they are. The mineral realm diffuses itself according to higher intelligence in what we understand to be the plant world. The plant realm embodies all of the intelligence of the mineral realm but adds a factor that is not observable in the lower order of things. Within the intelligence of the realm of plants there is added the factor of "reproducibility." After its kind, an apple is an apple and it is within itself capable of reproducing itself in keeping with its inherent intelligence. Each of the species of the plant realm has its own particular identity and it too must conform to its plan of being, though it could be said that it has not perceived of its identity.

The plant world diffuses itself according to a higher intelligence into the animal world. As in their earlier progressions of development or evolution, there is inherent in the animal realm all of the intelligence of both the plant realm and the mineral realm, except that here again there is a slightly more complex, added feature. In the animal kingdom we have the addition of mobility and instinct. Mobility and instinct seem to exist on this higher level in order to insure self-protection and heightened evolution of the species through survival of the fittest. In each of these realms there can be observed degrees of evolution as a result of the absorption of "lower level intelligence" into a higher, more refined intelligence. In any one of these realms we can observe degrees of evolution that are particularly significant. The amoeba is at a different level of development than is the chimpanzee.

As in the previous steps in evolution, the animal kingdom is diffused into the human world by virtue of a higher intelligence. In humankind there is embodied all of the intelligence of the lower orders in keeping with a higher, more complex intelligence. Here again there is a new, additional factor that makes a significant difference. Humankind has the added advantage of rational thought. That we can perceive the differences herein considered sets us far, far apart from our fellow creatures on this earth plane. Out of rational thought have evolved the increasingly complex systems of art, philosophy, theology, and (broadly) science. This would, of course, include all of the sciences and the descriptive and functional forms that make them discernible.

The power of rational thought has brought humankind to a perception of a link between his belief in deity and his expanding understanding of who and what he is, where he came from, and ultimately, where he is going. All the steps along his eternal way have been appropriate and logical. They have been neither good nor bad, simply a necessary part of his reason for existence. By virtue of a higher intelligence, humankind is diffused into what we may call the "spiritual world." This is *not* to be confused with what many people today mean by a "spirit world." The common conception of the spirit world is that of a realm of disembodied spirits, a geographically locatable place where the eternal part (soul) of us goes after the transition we call death. In the logical sequence of thought that we are following here, we conceive of the spiritual world as being that higher realm of our true self that is observable as a result of our perception of ourself as being something more than just human. A higher intelligence reveals to us that there must be reason for existence and orderly progression toward a higher goal.

At each step along the way of our eternal progression, there has been an activity of a higher intelligence that has caused us to move up along an intelligent, orderly pathway that leads us not only to where we are as an integral part of the spiritual realm, but on into misty, not-yet-discernible heights that have yet to be revealed. What is this ever-present "higher intelligence" that has functioned and still functions on all levels? What is this greater "knowing," this infinitely perfecting intelligence that must surely be at work right now moving us almost imperceptibly along an upward path? Surely it is that I AM inherent in us and everywhere equally present that has led us from kingdom to kingdom. Our perception of that I AM is the power by which we move assuredly into the spiritual realm of dominion and authority.

The spiritual world is that state of consciousness and its demonstration of awareness of oneness, unity. It is that degree of intelligence that gives us a new dimension of dominion and authority. It is one more magnificent step toward the full, intended, willed awareness of ourself as God expressed, according to our present consciousness of God. Here in this expanded realm we can move out of not knowing who and what we are, where we have come from and where we are going, into a realm of knowing the Truth—a knowledge of which, we are promised, will set us free. Isn't it a beautiful thought that at each step along our eternal pathway we have been given always a little more freedom? How exciting to get just a glimpse of that yet unnamed kingdom that lies ahead! It is a kingdom, however, that lies within, and must not be seen as an "otherworldly" kingdom in which we are not intimately involved.

Inherent within the traditional teachings of Christianity there is a strong belief that God is "the creator, the First Cause, the Deity," and that we as men and women are "the created, the result." There is a great (mostly unconscious) security in this concept. We are all too aware of our humanness, of our limitations. We have seen, all too clearly, our own fears as they demonstrate the need to compete with one another on all levels of human relationships. Our heritage and we individually have conditioned ourself to believe in our inadequacy in meeting the daily challenges that arise out of our need for one another. We have observed and even learned to measure accurately the aging process that causes us to accept limitations in our mental agility, our physical prowess, and our recuperative powers. Simply because a certain amount of time has passed, certain debilitation is presupposed to have occurred. We are unable, as a rule, to understand intellectually why we are here, where we came from, and what lies ahead of us; and that "not knowing" creates in us an anguish that frequently produces a sense of desperation. We feel trapped in the materiality to which we live in bondage. Even if we are blessed with enough or more than enough of this world's goods, the entire system of values based upon materiality harbors the dread of possibility of loss of supply. If we have never seemed to have enough or if we have lived in a demonstration of poverty, then we live momently with the agony of loss, of being left without.

When we wisely "face the facts," or "see it like it is" and "tell it like it is," the insecurity within us can be monumental. Though we may "put on a happy face," divert our attention by laughing a lot, drinking too much, burying ourself in a book, or watching television hour after hour, we still come back to that unspeakable insecurity that our world of humanness imposes upon us. For a time we may convince ourself that at the bottom of a bottle there is surcease, or that "speed," "grass," "uppers," or "downers" will set us free, but we keep coming back to the abysmal sense of hopelessness to which we might all be subject.

The belief that God the Creator (as distinguishable from humanity, the creator) is somehow above all this frightful inadequacy is a welcome, strengthening concept. But surely we can see that this concept still smacks of "otherworldliness." So long as we can be comfortable with the belief in something separate, even though we dimly see it to be divine, as being a solution to our desperation, we put off accepting our responsibility to grow and attain our promised dominion and authority. The belief in the "other-worldliness" of God, His anthropomorphic superiority, may make us feel good about our respect or adoration of deity, but it is no less an opiate for the agonizing pain that our separateness causes. An aspirin is a good thing, for it may take away the headache that is caused by the tension built up in human relationships, but until we resolve the conditions that produce the tension that causes the headache, we are not really experiencing the growth that is needed (as heralded by the headache). A belief in a superior, set-apart, and distinguishable-from-humanity God feels good, because it eases our human feelings of guilt that accompany our awareness of inadequacy. This good feeling is supported by the system of values that has grown out of our Judeo-Christian heritage. It is no less an opiate, however, than social drinking or the chemical adjustment that is supported by the system of values that has grown out of our materialistic society. There are many intelligent, good people who honestly believe in the acceptability of a martini or two, or a tranquilizer, as a solution to our twentieth-century agonies. There are many, many good and intelligent people who quite honestly and understandably believe that a God apart, superior to and different from us, is a valid concept, because it makes them feel better for a time. Our good Christian sensibilities may be shaken by such a comparison, but before we cast it out as blasphemous, let's take the time to think it through. After all, if our anthropomorphic God is wise and loving, surely He will not excommunicate us for an honest search for Truth! After all, His Son is recorded as having said, "You will know the truth, and the truth will make you free." The spiritual quest upon which we have ventured is a search for an awareness of the truth.

The truth is that there is only one Presence and one Power in the universe, and that allness and onliness is the reality that we can define as God—the one transcendent God that is both absolute, abstract principle and warm, real, loving, personal Father-Mother. The One, the Omnipresence, the Omnipotence, the Omniscience is to us (as we have a realization of It) a very real Presence. We may, as we continue to retain the residue of a belief in our humanness and therefore limitation, see this personal God as the "God of our fathers," the "Father-Mother God," our heavenly Father. We may find comfort and assurance in seeing this God as "Him," as His Son, Jesus Christ. There are many sincere, honest, intelligent, good people who cannot be faulted in their quest that has brought them to an acceptance of Jesus. They accost us on the street or in the market or at our door and inquire after our salvation, for they believe that the acceptance of this "otherworldly" personification of the one God, manifest as Jesus, is the way to salvation. Such good Christians must be praised for the commitment they honestly feel and for their desire to "witness" for their Lord and God.

Perhaps one of the most unfortunate side effects of such a belief is the attendant need to make a judgment of comparison. The result is that there would appear to be some who are saved and some who are not . . . some good, some evil. The embracing of yet another manifestation of duality and separation is unavoidable, for there is the *good* state of salvation and the *evil* state of desolation. If there is only one Presence and Power, God the good, then it is inconceivable that there could be a reality of desolation. How wonderful it would be if we could grow to the realization that in truth it is not necessary to make judgments based upon the erroneous belief in duality—in good and evil.

The concept of good and evil—of deity and devil, of heaven and hell—that we are urged to grow out of is not in itself either good or evil. After all, mankind has evolved the wisdom to perfect itself by the exercise of choice. We must grow beyond the belief, however, that that which is not chosen is intrinsically bad or evil. We must feel a great sense of gratitude to that infinite Knowing that is God for the insight to be selective and arrive at our own realization of ever-evolving Truth that brings us always closer to our ideal goal. A part of that process is awareness of and limitation by fear. We have feared the power of destructive forces that we have believed in and given names to. Eons ago, we called these Gods of evil or destruction, Satan or the Devil, and their place of residence a hell of damnation and destruction. The very belief in the personification of evil has evolved the fear that over the ages has created selectivity in us. Let us not make the mistake of condemning the traditional belief in God and Satan, heaven and hell,

26

good and evil. Rather, let us be wise enough to see them as integral parts of the wonderful growing process by which we fulfill our divine purpose in life.

CHAPTER IV

Surely one of the greatest challenges we have is in itself not a thing, not a reality. It is the fact of not knowing. Not knowing has such apparent reality that it almost takes on a personality of its own. A small child often frustrates his elders by his incessant questioning: "What is that?" "Where did I come from?" "Why?" "What does God look like?" "When are we going to get there?" "How long is forever?" "How can there be a tree in a tiny seed?" "What is love and where did it come from?" "Who?" "When?" "Where?" The child has no difficulty in dealing with his not knowing. None, that is, until he equates not knowing with that which is not chosen, and therefore undesirable or evil. Then he begins to feel guilty because he recognizes his own not knowing, but cannot perceive of his elders not knowing. After all, they have had forever to learn how to act as if they know it all.

The teenager is thrust into an almost untenable position. He is acutely and often painfully aware of his not knowing at a point when, through the natural process of selectivity, he is trying to make the choice between the naivete of childhood which he disparages for all he is worth, and what would appear to him to be the all-knowing of adulthood that he is trying so hard to emulate. Because he does not have the experience of a long life and its storehouse of knowledge, he gives in often to drugs, to unreasonable fantasy, to rejection of standards that his elders seem impelled to thrust upon him, or to suicide. His not knowing becomes a hated, feared burden—so heavy that often he cannot bear it. Having forgotten so quickly, the adult world slips easily into the pitfall of choice which reasons logically that the teenager (or at least his choices) must be evil. No wonder so many young people look with incredulity at our belief in Jesus or God, which seems not to have given us any discernible relief from the burden of not knowing.

Not knowing is no less a burden for the adult mind. The only difference is that we develop a stagnating indifference that keeps echoing, "Oh, what's the use!" Then we go to ridiculous ends to pretend that we really are know-it-alls, for the benefit of the rest of the world, which we somehow feel does know a bit more than we do. We can't face our not knowing, and we delude ourself by the many games we play. We give almost physical form to our "otherworldly" God or Jesus. Or we keep ourself dulled by the contents of all sorts and sizes of bottles so readily available to respectable adults. In order to keep up the pretense, we impose our delusions on our children as well as on one another.

This un-thing that seems such a burden is not knowing who and what we are. It is not knowing where we came from or where we are headed. Because of our not knowing, we are uncertain about the nature of deity, just as most of us have been since the dawn of civilization. Our not knowing produces serious, disturbing questions about life and its meaning. It causes us to fear death and those circumstances that we have come to believe are responsible for death. Not knowing makes us unsure of ourself in our relations with others. Because of our not knowing, we allow ourself to be made to believe that we are superior or inferior to others. We convince ourself that we must either dominate the other or be dominated by him. Because of not knowing, we have come to believe that it is only by our labor, our investment, and our saving "for a rainy day" that we can be assured of having what we need in the way of things on this earth plane.

We have sought to overcome our not knowing by turning to religion in one form or another, to education, and then to its offspring, science. We were, of course, right in the first place—or nearly right. We instinctively turned Godward but got caught up in the "otherworldliness" that had become our burden. You see, our not knowing is really an illusion, because we have never ever been separated from the knowing; we have only forgotten. That is a tremendous revelation: we don't have to go anywhere or be anything different than what we are, for the knowing, the Truth, is not far away. It is right here where we are, right now.

There is only God! God is all; all is God. We are God. We are not gods, separate from one another, we *are* God. There is only one Presence. That Omnipresence is God—infinite, absolute, impersonal God. We are that Presence, for there is no place that God is not. We live and move and have our being in Him—in that perfect, absolute, impersonal All. Stop now, and put this book down. Get still. Relax. Say to yourself slowly and quietly: "There is only God! God is all; all is God. I am God. I am not a god—I *am* God. There is only one Presence. That Omnipresence is God—infinite, absolute, impersonal God. I am that Presence, for there is no place that God is not. I live and move and have my being in Him—in that perfect, absolute, impersonal All." Now read those words again and center your thought in this eternal Truth.

As we come into a realization of this Truth, our not knowing will begin to lose its grip on us. Like physical darkness, not knowing is a nothing, an un-thing. Light doesn't have to struggle with darkness to overcome it; it has only to shine. We don't have to struggle with not knowing; we have only to see, to know, and to feel this Truth, and our not knowing will dissolve into its native nothingness. If we would set aside a time each day just to know this Truth, it would bring such light into our whole being! We must not argue with our historical or cultural or traditional beliefs. We need only to leave them alone, and know. We don't have to be able to explain to ourself, let alone anyone else, until we are filled with the light of knowing.

We are God; we came out of all that God is, and we continue to dwell in God. In the beginning (whatever that means) God was—God is. God conceived of His own idea of Himself—His only begotten Son. That was "at a time" so long as we continue to think in terms of time. But that beginning is now and tomorrow as well. We may have a little difficulty with this time concept, and if so, we should just leave it—if it is Truth, it will reveal itself in due course. We were (we are) formed out of the only substance there is—God substance. That substance is infinite, without limit. The portion of us that we recognize is not set apart out of this substance; it *is* this substance, and the extent of us does not limit this substance, for it is beyond our reach just as it is us.

The perfect plan of us is God's perfect idea of Himself. We are His only begotten. We may not know that we are; we may not look like or act like the only begotten, but we are that pure, perfect idea, and we are here to come into a realization of that perfect man-woman idea as a result of our willing to do so. Historically, as a result of our burden of "otherworldliness," we have assumed that Jesus Christ, the historical man Jesus, was the only begotten. Jesus the man put on the Christ when He came into the realization that He was the only begotten—God's perfect idea of Himself. He said, "I and the Father are one." When we come into the realization of the Truth that we are that pure, perfect idea, we too shall put on the Christ.

Along the path to putting on the Christ, we must come to realize that we are that perfect plan, that perfect knowing, that perfect wisdom expressing itself as us—according to our consciousness of it. We have always seemed to degrade wisdom by equating it with knowledge or awareness of it. Our knowledge or awareness of wisdom certainly is limited, but that limitation in no way degrades or limits wisdom. The principles of aerodynamics are a part of wisdom. Man's not knowing that part of wisdom in no way diminishes the wisdom. For the centuries and centuries during which man was unaware of the principles of aerodynamics, they still existed and were in no way limited by man's not knowing. When man discovered or became aware of the principles that had always been there, they immediately began to function for him. Though for centuries and centuries it was a *fact* that man could not fly, at no time was it *true* that he could not fly. The principles of aerodynamics existed as truly in the tenth century before Christ as they do in the twentieth century. The only difference is that in the twentieth century we came to know and therefore to apply these principles.

Is it not reasonable to state that in the tenth century before Christ, or in the eighteenth or nineteenth century after Christ, man was in truth able to fly, though his not knowing produced the fact of his inability? Since we are one with all wisdom, as a corollary of the Truth that God is wisdom, everywhere equally present, can we not see that we are wisdom in spite of the fact of our ignorance or not knowing? Regardless of our doubts and fears and the enormity of our not knowing, we are God expressing Himself as wisdom, as us, according to our consciousness of wisdom. As our consciousness of this truth expands, our applicability of infinite wisdom expands. We can see the evidence of this explosion of awareness of wisdom all around us. Just in one area alone—the field of communication—we have uncovered, discovered, remembered so much that has changed our life-style that it would be staggering to someone from the nineteenth century. Our children have so much more information and awareness to deal with than we had. Because we are dealing constructively with our not knowing, coming into an increasing awareness of who and what we are, it is safe to assume that the growth will continue to multiply itself. It will be exciting to see what our life-style will be in twenty or fifty more years!

CHAPTER V

As we pursue this exciting train of thought, can we conceive of ourself as being God expressing Himself as us, as life, according to our consciousness of life? To do so, it will be necessary for us to alter our concept of life rather radically. Because of our not knowing we have believed life to be limited to that animation that occurs between birth and death. Life is that quality that is characterized by growth, change, and interaction. Life is a quality that, by its very nature, cannot cease to exist. It may and does alter its expression, but it does not cease to be. Within the limitations of our not knowing we have used the concept of life to define a portion or limited expression of life—our material existence. Life, however, transcends this limitation, for the very essence of the universe and everything therein is the life-force, spirit. It is, like wisdom, everywhere equally present in all and through all.

Life is a process that is characterized by a constant activity of drawing together and unifying substance and wisdom in ever new and useful forms, and equally a process of separating and distributing substance and wisdom to allow a constancy of growth and change. A seed drops into fertile soil, and the life-force in it and around it (as soil, air, and water) moves to draw to it substance according to its inherent wisdom or plan or genetic structure. It sprouts and continues to draw to it what is needful to fulfill its divine pattern. It flowers and fruits and allows its seed to begin the process anew. The flower "dies," in so doing becoming the fruit. The fruit "dies," in so doing becoming the seed. The seed "dies" and becomes the recommencement of the entire process.

Humankind is part of the same kind of process. Science has revealed the fantastic journey upon which the infinitesimal sperm cell is launched, through a totally hostile environment, to find its way to the ovum. The life-force, motivated by an infinite wisdom in this process, causes this microscopic union. Out of itself and its environment, that union draws to it the energy and substance needful to form a new being according to its genetic plan. Prior to and long after the phase we call birth, this marvelous process goes on. The whole physical being draws from itself and its environment all that is needed to take on the stature that has always been there, in the midst of the process. Shoes no longer fit, trouser legs become too short, and blouses become too tight.

It is not only in the physical form that man experiences this miraculous metamorphosis—he changes too from day to day in his awareness of his environment and of himself. The eager and receptive mind is ever inquisitive, and gradually develops awareness, understanding, and skill. Through each sense individually and through all the senses in their combinations, man receives input or data, which he constantly evaluates, absorbs, or rejects. With every sensory response that reaches his brain, man changes—he is constantly different from ever before or any other.

Life is a drawing, gathering, unifying process that functions in accord with a most remarkable, inherent intelligence.

Over the passage of the hundreds of thousands of years that are involved, plant life fulfills its life cycle time after time. By the erosion of time, tide, volcanic action, and the like, layers of decaying plant life are deposited and covered. They "draw to themselves" intense pressure and then lie dormant to await their discovery as oil or coal by a "higher intelligence." The process goes on and on.

The process that is life is not limited to an accumulative activity; it also (and at the same time) causes a breaking down, a separating, a distributing of that which is inherent in form. Life in its fuller sense is everywhere equally present in all things. There is no place where life is not, because God is life and God, as we have postulated and come to understand, is Omnipresence. Now we see that God is also Omnipotent: all power, all movement, all change, all growth, all birth, and all death. That which we call death is (in the broadest sense) simply that point in the life process when the direction of the force is reversed. Death, a phenomenon that has been conceived by our not knowing, is as much a part of life as birth is. Because of our preoccupation with the material, the physical, we have assumed that birth occurs at that instance of emergence from the mother's body or separation from the forming body. In the light of our consideration here, how can we be so precise and assume that gestation is not a part of birth, or that the growing process that produces teeth or strength to walk is not a part of birth? In its broader sense, birth is a constant, continuous process in every form.

Surely this is also true regarding death. We commonly pinpoint death as occurring "when the vital life signs stop," when the heart stops beating, or when we stop breathing. However, if death is understood to be a part of the process of life that is characterized by the changing process of breaking down form and distributing substance, we must come to see that *death is life,* a continuing process. Death is inherent in life as the body casts off fingernail tissue or skin tissue, or when it decomposes in the earth or in the retort of a crematorium. Death must be as natural as birth. Neither is good nor bad; both are simply part of a miraculous process that moves us toward attainment of our goal of total, willed self-awareness.

In the evolution into the "spiritual world," the great added factor that sets us apart from simple human form, animal form, plant form, or mineral form is self-consciousness. Now obviously we are not referring here to discomfort born of embarrassment, but rather, consciousness of self-awareness of identity. Humankind seems to become capable of perceiving identity quite differently than do the "lower forms." In the lower forms, instinct allows species to "understand" themselves to be birds, or dogs, or lions, or reptiles. In the human world, man perceives his identity, but only in part. The process of perception of identity seems to develop from without to within.

We have become conscious of our identity (beyond the instinctive awareness of ourself as a human being) by recognizing that we have certain physical attributes that have made it possible for us to survive on this planet and to attain a degree of the dominance to which we all aspire. Our need to be dominant seems to transcend our instinct for the preservation of our species. It would seem that we are the only species with an instinct for the preservation of ideals. This causes us to be willing, even eager sometimes, to give up our life experience in favor of an ideal. Obviously, along with this we have developed a rationale that permits or drives us toward overemphasis on the worth of materialistic values. This rationale causes us to enter into conflict on a personal level and on a group level. We are the only creatures that go to war. All other creatures kill in order to eat or to keep from being eaten, but we as creatures have even gone so far as to create a science of war.

Because of our overemphasis on materialism, in our not knowing, we give expression to the creative drive that is in us in material forms. From earliest times, men have fashioned ideas into material form. On the walls of caves that have existed for hundreds of thousands of years, we find primitive markings and carvings that were the earliest expression of ideas in concrete form. We have no awareness of any other species that has developed this need or skill. Because of the loving, giving nature of a dear friend, I have a terra-cotta figurine, fashioned by man some time between 535 and 485 B.C. It is a burial figure that was placed in the tomb of a priest in ancient Egypt. Because of its original purpose and because of its antiquity, it is a valuable, beautiful piece of art. It is much more than that, however: it is the material outpicturing of a rather complex system of ideals, and an outstanding example of skill in the hands and eyes and judgment of a man in response to that system of ideals.

It would seem reasonable to assume that man did

not understand the drive within himself that manifested as creative art. It was simply a part of the process that would ultimately bring him to an awareness of spirituality as a reality within himself. The artist, the poet, the composer, the construction engineer are all people who are responding to the spiritually instinctive drive to create, to fashion anew the bounty of materiality into a higher, finer, more valuable or more useful form. It is this very drive that had drawn us into an awareness of values within ourself that permit us to transcend the materiality in which we live. During the dreadful days and nights of incessant bombing in Germany during World War II, ordinary people were able to live through the holocaust by listening to the music of great masters such as Wagner. In times of greatest trial, men have brought forth their most beautiful, most valuable and useful forms.

During the last twelve to fifteen centuries, we have brought our artistic heritage forward in the form of the sciences which have given us degrees of dominion and authority over the material world that were never dreamed of before. These sciences too have helped us to become aware of areas of reality that had been either lost to us or so hidden by our not knowing that we lived in poverty of mind and soul for centuries. It will take time for science to prove the insights of inspired souls down through the ages, but those insights are rapidly becoming the domain of ordinary men. No longer is the wisdom of the ages to be hidden from all but the few. Man's evolution into an awareness of himself as a real and living part of all that God is, is opening the door in consciousness that will allow a flood of insight and ever greater dominion and authority here and now. The alert and aware observer must be able to perceive—in the great strides man has made in the conquest of his planet Earth, his conquest of space, and his increased understanding of himself—a prelude to the revelation of himself as an expression of God. We are now mightily at the task of the conquest of inner space. It will be exciting to see what we accomplish in the next twenty or fifty years, won't it?

CHAPTER VI

At this point it is important for us to move logically into an awareness of the implied truth that we as human beings are something more than physical creatures. That the physical body is subject to the life process we call death is not in dispute. Once we really understand that death is a natural part of life, we can be set free from the fear of death that is so prevalent in our not knowing. It is not possible for us to be separated from God, His wisdom, life, love, and power. Instinctively we know that we are more than our body. Quite rightly, we function all the time as an entity that has a body, lives in a body, and uses the body for a period of time. We refer to our body, its parts and its functions, in an objective sense. *"My right hand is stronger and more accurately coordinated than my left hand." "My digestive system just will not tolerate overeating."*

The "I" of us is often hopeful about our body, or fearful about it. The "I" of us often wants to do things that our body seems incapable of doing. Anyone who has learned to type or operate an adding machine or play the piano has been acutely aware of the separateness of the "I" that aspires to become proficient and the fingers that strike the wrong keys. But with tenacity, the "I" of us is dominant. Because the "I" of us accepts the limitations of not knowing, we frequently fall short of the degree of proficiency to which we aspire. Ideally, however, the "I" of us is dominant. To the degree that we fail to maintain our dominance, we experience once again the frustration of not knowing.

The "I" of us is the part that is not limited by either the building-up process of life or the breaking-down part. Throughout the building-up process, it is reasonable to assume that the "I" of us remains relatively untouched by the process. The "I" of us is that sense or degree of awareness of identity. We can define that eternal part of us as the soul. The soul of us is the real or eternal part that existed before birth and surely exists after death. After the full cycle of seed, sprout, tree, flower, and fruit, the new seed in the fruit falls to the ground and "dies," but surely that is not the end of the identity of the seed. It simply begins anew the birth-death cycle that is in conformity with its inherent intelligence.

Man is a soul. You are a soul, I am a soul, every man, woman, and child is a soul. Each soul is a state of consciousness. Each soul is the sum total of all of the awareness that has within itself come into expression. The soul is made up of all the ideas, accurate or inaccurate thoughts, which we as identities have perceived. The soul is made up of all our feelings, reactions, evaluations, perceptions, and conceptions. The soul is the sum total of all the input that we as an individual identity have received. We have received that input from the perfect knowing of infinite Mind (God) that is everywhere equally present, and we have received input from our environment through our senses. Our perception of all to which we have been exposed is yet another factor, because we are constantly making deductions—accurate and inaccurate deductions—from what we know and sense.

If it were possible to evaluate all the input that makes up our soul, our consciousness, on a scale of one to ten, from accurate to inaccurate, we would be able to evaluate our soul and thus determine where we are on the road to full Self-consciousness. The sum total of our consciousness or soul is the determining factor for the kind of world, the kind of environment we are producing. You see, it is the soul that is responsible for all that we are manifesting at any point. The soul is the "I" of us that is ever on the pathway of unfolding our inherent, perfect pattern. God's perfect idea of Himself, His only begotten Son, is inherent within the soul and is, according to our awareness of it, now being expressed.

As an eternal soul, our purpose for existence is to come consciously and intentionally into an awareness, a full and complete awareness, of who and what we are. We have already postulated that we are God, expressing Himself as us, according to our consciousness, at any particular time. It is the will of God, the highest intelligence of God, that we should come to know the truth of our being . . . our being God. "You will know the truth, and the truth will make you free." But the truth does not make us free; it is the knowing of the truth that makes us free. It is our purpose to know the truth, intentionally, willingly, and willfully. At that point in soul evolution that is symbolically referred to in our Scripture as the creation, in Genesis, we were given dominion and authority; we were created in the image and after the likeness of God.

45

For a good many centuries now, in the light of scientific knowledge, it has been difficult for men to relate the Biblical stories of creation to what logic and reason seem to dictate. Yet there should be no difficulty if we begin with the premise (previously postulated) that there is only one Presence and one Power, God, the good, and then realize that Scripture is both mystical and apocalyptic. Throughout the centuries that Scripture has been evaluated by sincere seekers after truth, historians have, out of respect, placed the Bible in history, but have had considerable difficulty in finding historical authenticity in the Bible. The problems of overlapping and the considerable gaps that are evident make it difficult to find any historical validity in Scripture. That very suggestion causes a great many good Christians to bristle, because our Christian heritage has led us to believe that Holy Scripture is the word of God . . . that is, a verbal communication from an anthropomorphic deity. God, infinite Intelligence that is everywhere equally present, is the Truth of the universe. As man has evolved in his awareness of his interinvolvement in that Truth, he has perceived of degrees or portions of the truth, and the validity of this perception has caused him to endow his awareness of the Truth with a mystical significance. The Bible is that awareness that has become a tradition over the centuries. As such, it has taken on a personality of its own. Scripture, in and of itself, is neither good nor bad; it is just Scripture. Man has perceived of Truth and has handed down from generation to generation the mystical, apocalyptic stories of his perception and the circumstances out of which that perception arose. At some undefinable point in history, man began to endow that tradition with a sense of awe and adoration that unintentionally has set that tradition apart from him, thus adding to his sense of separateness.

In every other area of research and interest, man has not allowed himself to give undue importance and significance to his early discoveries. He has always moved on to perceive the greater discoveries and their awareness that awaited him, simply because he had made the previous discoveries. It would seem that in the area of religion and the study of spiritual truths, man has bogged down in worship of an early discovery rather than moving on to the greater truths that await him. As a result there is an adoration of the Bible itself, apart from what it conveys to us.

Let us move on in our awareness of Truth, that we might grasp an ever greater realization and thus fulfill the purpose of our existence. It has been recognized by Bible authorities that the first announcement in Scripture is perhaps the greatest that can be uttered—the fact of the being and creative power of God. The Bible begins with the truth of God. It begins with the recognition that God is ... that God exists, that there is one God, that He is the Creator of the universe and out of Him all else has evolved ... out of the allness and onliness of God. The universe is not self-existent. The same is true of man. Man was not only made by God, but in the image of God. Man is the supreme creative act of God. Man is coming to know and manifest his divinity and inseparable unity with God.

"In the beginning God ... " Not God and something else, not God and some time and space, not God and the basic elements of the universe, not God and anything! "In the beginning God ... " "And the earth was without form and void, and darkness was

47

upon the face of the deep." God is the uncreated, transcendent source of all being and all existence. All that proceeds out of or from God is of God. All is God, and God is all.

In the first and second chapters of Genesis there are two accounts of the creation. In the first, most often quoted, the order of creation places man as the final or ultimate creation. The second account places man in the primary position of creation, followed by the plant and animal realms. The apparent conflict here need not in any way detract from the importance, significance, and validity of Scripture, but rather it can open for us a whole new vista of awareness that can assist us in our quest for awareness of Truth. Bible scholars are pretty well agreed that the Scriptures as a whole (and these early passages in Genesis in particular) are the product of more than one human vehicle expressing out of his own inspiration. The infinite intelligence that is God inspires the receptive consciousness with truth, and that truth is then expressed according to the consciousness, or degree of awareness, of the vehicle.

Is it not reasonable to perceive that God conceived of Himself, begat His own and only perfect Man-Idea, and then proceeded in an orderly fashion to evolve that out of which the perfect Man-Idea could be manifest? Scripture (that is, our Scriptural tradition) expresses this truth in a mystical and apocalyptic fashion, using the words and ideas available to man in his present understanding: "Then the Lord God formed man of dust from the ground, and breathed into his nostrils the breath of life; and man became a living being." Remember, "In the beginning God . . . ," not God and something else. Therefore out of God, which was (and is) all that there was, God formed man, out of the finest substance, and "breathed into his nostrils the breath of life."

"And the Lord God planted a garden in Eden, in the East; and there he put the man whom he had formed." The perfect Man-Idea was created and then the orderly process for his manifestation was begun. The "days" of creation are in no way limited by time, but rather are the phases of the process in which all of us are now and ever shall be involved. This is not a description of an act in time, but the truth of an eternal process that causes the idea or ideal to progress to the manifest. This is what life is all about: the conception of an idea and its orderly progress to manifestation. We are God, expressing Himself as us according to our consciousness or awareness at this point in our perfect evolution toward unity.

The process that is spelled out apocalyptically in the story of creation is simple and clear. First there is the idea. Before anything can come forth into manifestation, there has to be an idea. The idea is eternal, not subject to the limitations of our power or ability to manifest it. All the forms of a perfect idea may come and go, they may be limited and imperfect in expression; but inherent within each one is the perfect idea, which remains perfect. The first step, the first day of creation, is of light. Can we not see that this is descriptive of the conception of the idea, the ideal? The second day of creation (the second step in the creative process) is the firmament, the environment in which the idea can move toward manifestation. On the third day in the story of creation, we see the third step in the creative process as the forming of the mineral and plant (or vegetable) realms. This is

49

the advancement of consciousness into ever higher degrees of intelligence in manifestation. Then there must be that which evidences the truth that in their separate forms there is still unity. Separation was not created to be seen as anything but a part of the greater whole. It was on the fourth day, in the fourth phase of creation, that the relationship between the forms and the universe at large was reaffirmed, in the establishment of the functions of the sun and moon.

The first four phases of the creative process can be defined as those pertaining to matter. Out of these evolves the "higher" intelligence or greater awareness that includes (on the fifth and sixth days) the forming of sea animals, the winged creatures, the beasts and cattle, and finally the forming of man. The seventh part of the creative process is the "day of rest," when that which has been created may draw to it all that is needed for its fulfillment in manifestation.

The Bible is, when rightly understood, the story of the unfolding of the consciousness of man. Because it comes to us out of antiquity, having been translated again and again by many levels of consciousness, from one language to another and from one culture to another, it is often difficult to be able to interpret Scripture and relate it to our everyday experience. Scripture reveals the evolution of the consciousness of man, from his origin in the Mind of God to his full willed and willful realization of Himself as God, as manifest in the Christ incarnate. Because of the awe of the Bible in which we stand, we will continue to return to it again and again until our expanding awareness causes it to reveal all its great insights. Our path on the journey to willed Self-awareness can be made clearer from time to time when we see the Bible as a road map that has led others before us. Perhaps the symbols on the map are not always clear to us, but if we keep returning to the proven value of the map, it will give up to us the insights that we are ready to grasp.

CHAPTER VII

One of the greatest hurdles to willed Self-awareness is the apparent dichotomy that exists, born of our relationship with other human beings. After we have arisen in consciousness to a point of Self-awareness . . . that is, when we come to the point in our evolution where we truly know who and what we are—we will come into the realization that there is really, totally, no such thing as separation. Until we come to that point, we must develop an understanding relationship with others that is compatible with the greater truths we are working toward.

It has often been said by the chauvinist in us that the only real problem that men have with women or women with men is that "you can't live with them and you can't live without them." That is a rather limited and negative expression, but it reveals a basic truth that must be understood. We need each other! More than that, we are eventually going to come to understand that others are more a part of us than are our hands or feet.

Oddly enough, even with our erroneous sense of separation from others, the overwhelming majority of our problems are the direct result of our inadequate handling of human relations. Broadly and generally speaking, the most common cause of inharmony in human relations is competition. Like virtually everything else in our world of separateness and not-knowing, there can be relative value to competition (even though here we are going to deal with its limiting aspects). Let us agree and establish that there are circumstances in which competition can be and is healthy. A spirit of competitiveness can and does cause us to reach greater heights, achieve greater degrees of efficiency, proficiency, and accomplishment. We can see it to be a positive factor in growth in many ways; nonetheless, a sense of competitiveness is the greatest cause of inharmonious human relationships.

Competition is as natural as being born without the developed skill of speech. As learning to speak is natural and appropriate, so also is growth out of competition. "When I was a child, I spoke like a child, I thought like a child, I reasoned like a child; when I became a man, I gave up childish ways." As we come into an awareness of our divinity, we come to realize that we have really only one appropriate area for competition, and that is in competing with ourself individually. We must continually better our record, for the law of growth is an immutable law. What we have accomplished today . . . the degree of our lovingness, the scope of our knowing, the breadth of our aliveness . . . these alone are worthy of competing with.

We begin early in life to become aware that others—mothers, fathers, sisters, and brothers—seem to have the power to keep our good or our desire from us, if not to take it away. We begin early in life to compete for living space, for food, for care and attention. Throughout our formative years we are constantly being encouraged to compete with one another, rather than with ourself. Because we fear there is not enough good to go around, we compete for our parents' approval and love. We compete for their time and attention. We compete with one another for the most-wanted toy, the biggest dish of ice cream, the most popular girl or boy, the top ten positions in class, the best-paying job, the most satisfaction and gratification in our personal relationships. We compete in the job market and around the bridge table; we compete for the rungs of the ladder of success and for the appreciation and plaudits of our peers. We compete for the attention and love of our children and our parents. We compete in conversation, and we compete around the dinner table and in bed. We compete for space on the road and in the line.

The staggering thing is that we haven't yet come to realize that no one or no thing can keep our good or our evil from us. The unrelenting activity of divine law is now, always has been and always will be, at work in us and around us. The law is absolute. According to our consciousness we experience the infinity or finiteness of the universe. According to our consciousness we draw to ourself bounty or deprivation, aliveness or stagnation, love or hatred, disease or perfectness, satisfaction or frustration, loneliness or affinity. Once we realize that all life is consciousness, we can no longer blame another for our limitations or imperfections. It is neither people nor times nor fate nor stars that determine the quality of our life experience . . . that is totally and directly due to our own consciousness. Our ethnic or national heritage can no longer claim responsibility or credit for what we are. It is not our parents or our family or our schooling, not our circumstances in any way, that are responsible for who and what we are manifesting at any point in time.

In order to be able to accept this truth and be set free by it, we must realize that each of us is an eternal soul. Our being is not limited by the brief time and experience that we refer to as "our life." The soul of man has experienced many, many lives. We have chosen the environment into which we were born by virtue of the consciousness that our eternal soul has attained. The soul that you are has traversed all the levels of consciousness that have equipped you with elemental and instinctive knowing. We have come into this life experience with millenniums of "knowing." We must, however, intentionally will to be aware of our infinite, spiritual heritage rather than accept only our purely human or physical heritage.

Many people express a remembrance of past lives. There are even those who feel that their psychic powers enable them to give life readings of the previous lives of others. Most of us have little or no recollection of any life experience beyond this one. If there is any recollection remaining after we are very small children, it is only fragmentary. This of course does not in any way detract from the reality of lives previously lived. If we have a progressive affinity with all life and we can come to accept the truth that death is not in any sense a finality, but rather a natural part of life, then reincarnation is a logical proposition.

Reincarnation is a concept that is disturbing to many people. The two most frequent reasons for being disturbed by the thought of reincarnation are that such a concept does not allow for ascension to a geographically locatable place called heaven at the conclusion of this life experience, and that it seems to preclude a meeting elsewhere with loved ones who have preceded us in death. Of course there is really a third reason for being disturbed by the thought of reincarnation: it is a concept that not only is not embraced by traditional Christianity, but is considered by much of traditional Christianity to be almost heretical. There still is in our Christian heritage much that tends to suggest that all Truth has already been discovered; if an idea is not popularly acceptable by theologians today, one who wishes to maintain a relationship with traditional Christianity would dare not give consideration to any such idea. The interesting thing is that Christianity came into being because Jesus of Nazareth had sufficient courage to be willing to consider that which might be considered blasphemous, to find a deeper insight into His relationship with God and share it with the world. He was sufficiently courageous to take His faith even to Calvary. But then, that was not so difficult for Him, since He was not burdened with not knowing as we seem to be.

For one who wishes to research the concept of reincarnation in greater depth, an excellent starting point would be the book "Reincarnation in World Thought" compiled and edited by Joseph Head and S.L. Cranston. The editors quote the British physicist, Raynor Johnson, from his work "The Imprisoned Splendour": "Some people seem curiously and almost instinctively interested in these topics [reincarnation and pre-existence]; others, frequently religious-minded people, feel antagonistic, as though some strange pagan faith were subtly menacing their cherished beliefs. The average thoughtful Western man has in general given little consideration to these matters, although his reticence does not always match his knowledge. In any attempt to formulate a philosophy of life and endeavor to see meaning in our pilgrimage, these ancient beliefs cannot be lightly set aside. It is our duty to weigh them carefully, and without prejudice, in order to see if they will illuminate for us tracts of experience which would otherwise remain dark and mysterious. . . . The idea of reincarnation presents no logical difficulties, whatever be the emotional reaction to it. What the soul has done once by the process of incarnation in a physical body, it can presumably do again.

"By the term 'soul'," Dr. Johnson explains, "we mean that individualized aspect of the Self, including . . . the Intuitive Self and Higher Mind, all of which are regarded as immortal. We should of course bear in mind that what is meant by the phrase 'have lived before' is not that the physical form (and personality) Raynor Johnson has lived on earth previously, but rather that Raynor Johnson is only a particular and temporary expression of an underlying immortal soul which has adopted previous and quite possibly different appearances."

In the preface of "Reincarnation in World Thought," the editors write: "Turning now for a moment to . . . sections on oriental religions, it seems essential to distinguish between the views of the great religious teachers included therein, and the later conventional emphasis on the attainment of the bliss and quietude of Nirvana as the supreme aim of man's incarnations on earth. There seems little psychological difference between the latter belief . . . perhaps a distortion of the real meaning of Nirvana . . . and the escape promised by Western religions, since in both instances the goal is usually a static state of happiness where striving and learning cease. If any religion encourages a race to heaven or Nirvana, the philosophy of reincarnation of course fails to communicate its central message of eternal growth. . . .

"Jung calls rebirth 'an affirmation that must be counted among the primordial affirmations of mankind . . . ' " This exhaustive treatise poses the questions: "How shall one regard the widespread current interest in the doctrine of many lives? Is it an apprehensive return to the thinking of a bygone age, a hopeless pursuit of lost securities? Or is it possibly an intuitive reaching out to repossess a heritage belonging to every man, now to be recovered at the level of both critical intelligence and affirmative daring?"

Our "non-escapist approach" necessitates a reevaluation of the concept of heaven and a thoughtful and considerate evaluation of our natural desire to have a continuing relationship with loved ones who have preceded us in death. We have previously postulated that our reason for existence is to come willingly and willfully into a state of total Self-consciousness—that is, to come to know fully that we are God, expressing Himself as us, and to realize and understand that we exist in unity with Him. Once we have come to realize that there is no separation, that there is only God, we will be ready to know that the insight of eons of time that has evolved the concept of heaven seeks to make us know that we are *now* in heaven . . . or in hell. There is no place that we are going to go to, for the very concept of space that puts you there and me

59

here and our "departed" loved ones out there is simply a part of our not knowing that we are, always have been and ever shall be, one with all that God is.

The word *heaven* has its root in the word *oranus,* which simply translated means expansiveness. Those of great insight down through the ages have perceived, though perhaps dimly, that after the experience we call death, the eternal soul, that individualized aspect of God as infinite and absolute Mind, moves on into an expansiveness (heaven) that offers beauty and joy and peace and loveliness beyond our present capacity to describe. As a result, in our inadequacy of description we have given physical dimensions to our concept of heaven by giving it pearly gates and golden streets. Perhaps the apostle John, the son of Zebedee, had reference to this divine expansiveness when he said: "See what love the Father has given us, that we should be called children of God; and so we are. The reason why the world does not know us is that it did not know him. Beloved, we are God's children now; it does not yet appear what we shall be, but we know that when he appears, we shall be like him, for we shall see him as he is."

When the allness and onliness of God does appear to our consciousness, we shall know that we dwell now in His eternality and no longer need the escapist concept of having to go somewhere. The truth is that we are now busy at the task of growing into an ever-expanding awareness of who and what we are, and all the while overcoming our not knowing. Isn't it a wonderfully comforting thought that right now you are, in spite of your not knowing, busy at being Being (God)? Right now your searching soul that has brought these pages into your hands is unfolding into the greater awareness of your divinity.

Of course, the acceptance of this kind of thought means that we must alter our belief about hell as well. The inspired people of antiquity tried within the limitations of their own inspiration (and the bountiful not knowing of their listeners) to explain that as we continue, for whatever reason, to refuse to grow, and thus stagnate in not knowing, we shall by our own action separate ourself from the growth process and experience a continuing torment. Hell is not a place to go to, but rather a state of consciousness that we now dwell in to some extent. The Christian concept of "heaven and hell" is a more dramatic development of our not knowing, but inherent within it is a hidden apocalyptic meaning that can lead us to greater freedom in Truth.

Surely one of the most beautiful facts of our existence here and now is that we do need one another; there is great joy and fulfillment in that dependency and the relationships that evolve out of it. The love, the sense of belonging to and possessing of one another, is certainly one of our most precious qualities. It is true that we cannot live without one another. We share deep and meaningful experiences that are beyond description, and each one makes us a living part of other souls. This is surely most appropriate, and one day it will be seen as one of the earliest and most significant expressions of our true unity with God. You see, all that we have considered about ourself and our relationship to God is equally true for everyone else. That is easy to understand about those for whom and from whom we have the expression of love, and perhaps a bit more difficult to understand regarding those with whom we have no conscious awareness or expression of love.

Those whom we have come to love are now and eternally a part of us, just as we are now and eternally a part of them. Regardless of what happens to them physically, we can never lose those we love. So often we hear references to those who have preceded us in death as "those we have lost," but that is totally inappropriate and inaccurate. You cannot lose anything or anyone you have loved. It is not possible. It is comforting to know that one who has gone on is, as we are, growing into a greater awareness of his unity with all that God is; and that along the pathway, whatever has made us one (love) will draw us together in yet another life experience that will be strengthened by our previous unity. We will "see" those whom we have loved in the ever-expanding realization of life. Just how we will know them is not yet revealed, but we *will* know them, for in truth, we are them and they are us. This may not be clear to us, for we see dimly yet, but the light is coming.

CHAPTER VIII

In addition to our normal or usual fears stemming from not knowing about freedom from cessation of life, there are a host of other misty, veiled fears that many of us have difficulty dealing with, which are related to belief in death as a reality. When we are in a positive, "up" flow of consciousness, it is generally much easier to go with a positive, "up" idea. "When the sun is shining, everything is beautiful!" However, when our train of thought is headed in the wrong direction and we are down in the dumps, things can get wholly out of proportion. The law of attraction can be seen at work in our thoughts, for when we get into a negative or unpleasant mood, we seem to draw more and more negative and unpleasant thoughts to deal with. Similarly, when we are "up" it seems as though nothing can go wrong.

In just the same way that we have collectively developed an "escapist approach" to life, we have done so individually. Our collective development of the escapist approach, as we have seen, has taken the form of a belief in (and therefore a striving toward) a static state of happiness where striving and learning cease. We have, in the Western world, termed this never-never land *heaven*, and we have conceived of a geographical place where we will be engowned and perhaps play some sort of ancient stringed instrument. The escapist approach to life is entirely understandable, in the light of our not knowing. Such a thought has surely served a worthwhile purpose in the evolution of our spiritual Self-consciousness. Like so many of our limited concepts, this is one that we must grow out of. Our age must give birth, not to an ancient wisdom but rather to a new wisdom.

Individually we have conceived of and developed all sorts of "escapes" from the pressures that beset us in our upward journey in overcoming our not knowing. One of the most familiar of these is the power of rationalization. We have mastered the fine art of rationalizing ourself into and out of all sorts of situations. The personal concept of a personal heaven or hell can be seen to be an unconscious act of "copping out," since it is here and now that we have the opportunity and the responsibility to grow. When we understand that there is no place where the God that we are is not, we can no longer rationalize a procrastinating belief in "otherworldliness" or "othertimeliness."

One alarmingly prevalent aspect of the escapist approach is the thought of suicide. Understandably, the disturbed, severely pressured mind that is groping in not knowing can give consideration to such a thought. There is not a one of us who has not thought about suicide as a possible retreat from the pressures of daily human experience. Perhaps most of us have not given it serious, extended, or consistent thought, but we have all considered it. Fortunately, most of us instinctively found serious consideration almost abhorrent. Nonetheless, though every instinct in us would reject the validity of such an approach, we can understand how one might not only give serious consideration to it but might (and often does) resort to suicide. An evidence of our maturity will be seen when we demonstrate that, although we would choose a different solution, we can and must understand and be understanding of the one who in his not knowing takes this path. If we can appreciate (though not approve of) such an act, not only can we be loving and understanding of another in his plight, but we can cause a great growing forth in our own consciousness. Because man can rationalize a static state of happiness where striving and learning cease, and because he can conceive of "othertimeliness," it is almost reasonable to assume that if the pressures of the moment became too great, we might consider or even perform the act of suicide. In the light of our quickening awareness that there is only one Presence and one Power in the universe—God, the good omnipotent, in whom we live and move and have our being—and that we *are* that Presence and Power now manifesting according to our consciousness at this moment, we must see that suicide is in no way an answer to any problem. If as we have postulated life is consciousness, then there is in our consciousness, in the realm of the ideal, the mind counterpart of everything, every circumstance and every condition in our life. That which has brought us to the point of suicide exists in consciousness as well as in fact. We as an eternal soul take with us from life experience to life experience all the factors of our soul or consciousness. That which has brought us to this point in our life experience is an integral part of the soul that is eternal.

It is important for us to understand that the fabric

of our soul is made up of all the growth, all the knowing, all the wisdom that we have become aware of to this point. It is also made up of those areas of consciousness that have not yet grown but are being readied for growth. So we have that which we have attained in consciousness, and the potential of that which we have yet to attain. Some people, burdened with not knowing, refer to that potential as evil or negation or unpleasant karma. It is in its simplest form just potential, neither good nor bad. Could it be said that the child who is just learning his numbers is evil or negative, to the extent that he has not yet learned addition or subtraction or division? Of course not! Simply because there is that in your consciousness or mine which is even now drawing experiences that will cause us to grow, even painfully, there is no logical or appropriate reason for assuming that it is evil or negative.

To refuse to meet the growth challenge that lies before us at any point in our eternal evolution to spiritual Self-awareness will in no way cause that challenge to cease to exist or go away. Each time we postpone the opportunity to grow, it becomes relatively more difficult and challenging to do so. Suicide is only a postponement of the inevitable. In the process of evolving an ever finer, more accurate way for mankind in its spiritual evolution, formal religion has laid a heavy burden on the soul of man. The one who chooses the path of suicide accomplishes nothing except the additional burden of self-recrimination.

A part of the newly acquired burden of guilt and recrimination and self-pity the victim of suicide accepts is the belief that God will be angry, offended, and filled with a spirit of vengeance. To many sincere,

66

good Christians the vision of a vengeful God is very real. In the confusion of our not knowing we have conceived of our God as an anthropomorphic being whom we think of as acting and reacting the way we would in our consciousness of not knowing. *God is love.* This great insight perceived by our elder Brother . . . that part of our infinity that has gone before us to show the way . . . can make us know that in this experience as in every other, God is eternally here, loving, forgiving, sustaining, and strengthening us in our inevitable progress toward our willed consciousness of being Being (God). Perhaps we can better understand this freeing truth if we go back to an earlier example, that of the laws of aerodynamics. Those laws did not get angry nor punish man because he did not understand. They were just there, patiently awaiting perception on the part of man. When we are ready to know the infinite love that God is, it will be there just waiting for our perception and our rejoicing in the freedom that it brings.

If you stop and think about it logically, there are two ways in which man commits suicide. He does so suddenly with the aid of a long drop, a gun, a razor blade, or an overdose of a harmful chemical substance, or he does so slowly and gradually over the extended period of most of his adult life. Because of our not knowing we have trapped ourself in what would appear to be "very real" material conditions that inhibit our spiritual growth. In one way or another our soul finds a way to release itself from the frustrating and painful conditions that are the direct result of our not knowing. Is the one who murders himself quickly any more wrong than the one who takes forty or fifty or sixty years to do so? How wonderful it would be if we could realize that we don't have to suffer the extended and lengthy pain of limitation or the sharp jerk of suicide. We can come to know our eternal oneness with all that God is and we can move easily and freely from one life experience to another, because we are never ever separated from the Presence and Power that God is as us, here and now manifesting according to our consciousness.

Perhaps we have known of those who chose the path of suicide; if they were close to us, family or friend, we too probably accepted a burden that in the light of Truth is totally inappropriate. The loved one who has chosen this path needs the strengthening effect of our faith in God as love, not our recrimination or pity or scorn or shame. Loose him and let him go. His soul, in his not knowing, has chosen this path, and he will come to know the Truth that will make him free, for he is now, always has been and always will be, one with the God of love that is everywhere equally present. The love that is God is loving him as He is loving you and me and every other soul that He is. How wonderful to know that we cannot be separated from all that God is! How wonderful to know that within us at any time we have the power and wisdom and faith and courage to meet the challenge of growth!

CHAPTER IX

In conceiving of ourself as being Being . . . as being God expressing Himself as us according to our consciousness . . . we come into a significant awareness of our importance individually. Such a conception could be the means by which we can set out on quite an ego trip! To many good, sincere Christians, the whole notion of such a consideration is blasphemous. In our not knowing we have tended over the ages of our evolution to put humanity down, simply because we were seeking to expand our consciousness of a divine potential. Trying to conceive of something greater, more expansive, and more nearly perfect, we have inadvertently concluded that the lesser is not good, and we have moved logically into a belief that humankind is evil. Since we have come to consider the allness and onliness of God, and our being an expression, a pressing out in form of God, we ought to risk the possibility of setting out on an ego trip, because the growth that surely will occur is a sufficiently precious prize.

We can avoid the danger of making this growth process an ego trip by realizing that what is true about us as we grow out of not knowing is true also about every other soul. It is true about us whether we have experienced more illumination than others along the way, or are still struggling under the burden of not knowing. It is true that we have developed all sorts of human, physical, mental, emotional, sexual, materialistic standards by which we can be set apart as superior to or inferior to one another. Part of our growth process is being able to see God in others. A vitally important part of this process is coming into the significant awareness of the importance of every human being, regardless of where our relative evaluation of him might place him. Every other human being is a living soul in the process of evolving spiritual Self-consciousness. All persons are God expressing Himself as them, according to their consciousness at any given point. Whether a person is good or bad, educated or uneducated, young or old, short or tall, black or white, he is God, for we must remember that there is only one Presence and one Power in the universe, God, the good.

Since the majority of our challenges as human beings are directly or indirectly involved in unsatisfactory human relationships, there must be here a considerable not knowing with which we are burdened. Throughout our life we have been and continue to be bombarded with an almost inescapable need to judge others, and a constant flow of differing values by which to judge them. From our earliest days in this life experience we have had models held up by which to make judgments. We have been taught "to hold your fork like Mommie does"; "be more like your big brother"; "trim and develop your figure like the current sex symbol"; "wear the manly scent like your favorite football star"; "eat the packaged food of the greatest athletes"; "drive the car that will make you popular with the girls"; "wear the right hosiery, and men will turn and follow you in the street." According to these outside pressures, it is absolutely vital for a woman to be either flat-chested or full-bosomed, regardless of her natural endowment, because clothes designers decree it. A man must grow a moustache or shave it off, wear a crewcut or a ponytail, or he will never make it with women or in the competitive world of commerce.

The basic forms of government by which the vast majority of human beings are governed are those that include a continuing process of judgment. We must determine from an early age whether others are good or bad, honest or dishonest, attractive or unattractive, desirable or undesirable, wise or foolish, kind or cruel. As we begin to evolve a consciousness of the infinity of God and our unity with that infinity, surely we must come to know that as we look at any other fellow human being we are looking into the face of God. In reality, others are not good or honest or attractive or desirable or wise or kind; they are simply God. They are God expressing Himself as them, according to their spiritual Self-awareness. Even though virtually everything in our human, materialistic world seems to belie it, we don't have to make relative judgments about others. After all, it is just those relative judgments that continue to set us apart, and in our separateness we breed discontent and inharmony.

Of course, here again we must see that there has been and is validity in our proclivity for judgment. Judgment, like sandpaper, is a contributing factor toward the polish that leads us onward, upward, and inward on our search for freedom from not knowing. Because we have made wiser, more loving and unifying judgments about our fellow human beings, not only have they progressed but we too have gained stature and strength, peace and poise.

Because of the standards that have been unconsciously thrust upon us or that we may have developed prayerfully and painfully for ourself, we frequently make limiting and unfortunate judgments. We judge that others are more attractive, more desirable, more in demand than we are, and in our not knowing we produce the acutely painful, totally irrational sense of jealousy. A small boy whose parents just couldn't afford a bike for Christmas was seen inspecting the one that a neighbor child got. Upon his return to his parents, his only comment was: "Jeff got a new bike for Christmas. It has dropped handlebars, ten-speed gears, and drinking bottles, but I wouldn't have it . . . it's blue!" It doesn't take much sensitivity to feel and understand the jealousy that the boy felt.

A hard-working junior executive strives, often at the expense of his family and his health, to come into line for the vital promotion that promises security, fulfillment, and ego satisfaction, only to see the promotion go to another who seems less qualified and deserving. The jealousy crisis into which he moves can (and often does) ruin his life. The mother of small children who seems trapped in her responsibilities and the demands they make upon her sees her life as drab and filled with drudgery. The fashion models, actresses, secretaries, and even salesclerks seem to lead charmed lives of excitement and color. When her husband comes home and seems to compare her unfavorably with her "more fortunate sisters" in the world, all reason begins to abandon her. "The green-eyed monster" rears its ugly head.

Jealousy is born of not knowing that no one can take our good from us. It is born of not knowing that by right of consciousness *we* determine our lot, not someone else. Because of our not knowing we have relegated to others the power of determination. We allow others—individuals, institutions, trends, governments, and professions—to determine our life-style, be it relatively good or bad. But we don't have to relegate this divine prerogative to others. Once we know that from the beginning of time we have been given dominion and authority over our life, we will be set free from the need to make judgments and from the attendant jealousy that is so destructive and painful.

There is another allied factor in not knowing which is either the product of jealousy or partly responsible for jealousy: the factor of possessiveness. Because we have not known the truth about ourself or others, because we have seen ourself in a competitive relationship with others, we have developed the need and the rationale for possessing others and being possessed by them. We physically give birth to another soul and from the instant of conception until the manifestation of separation by death, that child is "ours." "*My* baby is certainly kicking within me today!" "*No child of mine* is going to act like that!" "*I* give this bride in marriage."

Though perhaps to a lesser degree, each of us is always the child of his parents. No matter how old we become, what we accomplish with our life, to a certain extent we are always Mother's boy or Daddy's girl. It never seems to occur to us that this consciousness is an inappropriate one, which we must grow out of. Like virtually everything else that comes into our life, this possessiveness comes to pass . . . not to stay, but to pass. God grant that it should! Possessiveness certainly serves worthwhile purposes in our life. It is good that parents of small children and children of elderly parents care enough to possess, and in possessing to look after their loved ones when they seem unable to care for themselves.

In addition to the possessiveness present in varying degrees in virtually all of our other relationships—*my* neighbor, *my* secretary, *my* labor force, *my* boss, *my* co-workers, *my* enemies, *my* friends—we develop a unique and far-reaching degree of possessiveness in our love relationships. We think it's cute when a five-year-old speaks of *his* girl friend, or points out someone he will marry one day. As the mores of our society seem to change, our children begin "going steady" at ever earlier ages. Stop some day at a greeting-card rack in a department store and see how many cards convey the concept of *possession* of loved ones. Love and possessiveness are depicted as almost synonymous.

To be able adequately to appreciate our love relationships, let us see them in order as they express on the spiritual, emotional, mental, and physical levels. Our love relationships are so complex that they seem to defy understanding, let alone explanation! To the extent that we are evolved in our awareness of our unity with all souls, we develop love relationships with all souls. That is, we recognize in ever-increasing degree that spiritually there is no separation between us and others. We are in truth much more a part of all other souls than we are of our own hands and feet. We will at some point lay down this physical form, but we are eternally one with the soul of every other being. As we begin to perceive this we can recognize the importance of a conscious, willed love relationship with every expression of the God presence that we are. That which hurts any soul hurts each of us. Any growth, blessing, or benefit that any soul experiences brings me as soul into greater unity with all that God is. On the spiritual level, every love relationship we have with other souls is an edifying, unifying, harmonizing activity of God as love.

On the emotional level our love relationships seem to be almost involuntary. They are not, of course; they just seem that way. Because we have so little in the way of directional understanding of our emotions, it would appear that we are at the mercy of our feeling nature. Just what the chemistry is that produces our love relationships with one another is difficult to define. We spend the early part of our life evolving a standard or norm by which to judge our ideal kind of person, based upon physical attributes, mental attitudes, spiritual standards, and social refinements, only to find ourself almost involuntarily in an emotional love relationship with an entirely different kind of person. "I couldn't help falling in love with you." A love relationship with another on the emotional level is a complex feeling of attraction, a union or mating that is in no way dependent upon a response of any kind from the other. Such a relationship on the emotional level relies to a great degree upon our capacity to fantasize. The volatile, unbridled emotions of a teenager cause him to dream dreams of others and to have relationships within himself that can carry him to heights of ecstasy and depths of agony. He doesn't appear to have much

75

control over the comings and goings of these relationships, but in each one he has the opportunity to learn to direct his emotions through his responses. The adolescent girl who so deeply and so painfully loves her favorite rock or country-and-western star gains directive control of her feelings each time she rises to heights or plummets to depths of feeling.

It is really rather difficult to separate our love relationships on the emotional and mental levels, for the one is the vehicle of expression of the other. We mate on the intellectual level, and with each mating there is a broadening of our entire nature. In a very real sense, we become a part of the other person with each intellectual encounter. Where there is much in common between souls—that is, much in common on a conscious level—there is an observable dovetailing that works toward unity. The academic or formal learning years are times of deep and lasting love relationships on the mental or intellectual level.

Whereas on the spiritual, emotional, and mental levels of our love relationships we are dealing with ideals, feelings, and thoughts, on the physical level we incorporate these into dealing with our physical body. All the complexities of spiritual growth, emotional feelings, and mental attitudes are thrown into the need and desire to give physical expression to our love relationships. Because of our not knowing that each level of expression is as spiritual, divine, beautiful, appropriate, and acceptable as any other, we have developed standards of morality that demand consideration and possibly reevaluation.

As mankind conceived of and came to appreciate the various and complex levels of his experience and expression, he fell once again into competitive evaluation. The whole complex system of values that we have developed as we have grown toward Self-awareness (as we are using that term here) has, as we have seen previously, caused us to determine that some experiences, some attitudes, some powers, and some drives within us are good and some are evil. As we conceived of good *vs*. evil, we came to see these values manifest as deity *vs*. humanity. There was value in the concept of good and evil, and we have come to know deity and to see ourself as God expressing Himself as us, by conceiving of deity as distinct from humanity. We must, however, grow out of a competitive notion of judgment and no longer assume that if the one is good, the other is evil.

It has been this belief in the inherent evil of man that has been responsible for the creation of a system of moral values. Moral values are those which involve social approval or disapproval by reference to some standard outside the immediate issue. Primitive people were rarely concerned with the origin of such standards and the validity of judgments made by reference to them. They assumed that the standards were self-validating. It is only in fairly recent times that man has come to question the validity of the basic concepts upon which our morality has been based, the concepts of good and evil. Such questioning is clearly a part of the light or wisdom of our time. The possessiveness that is the natural result of our love relationships is like the concept of good and evil, which demands continuing consideration and reevaluation. It is in the area of physical expression or manifestation of our love relationships that possessiveness has been carried to its greatest extremes, and it is here, where it is most evident and most acute, that we may be able to deal with it and grow out of it.

CHAPTER X

Basically our love relationships involve the instinctive drive toward the perpetuation of our species that can be seen on every level of existence. All species have an instinctive drive toward reproduction. In mankind at least, there is added to this instinct a rationalization that has produced a refinement in relationships between the entities so involved. This rationalization has produced the concept of possessiveness with its positive and productive aftereffects, as well as its negative and limiting aftereffects. This has been responsible, in part at least, for the many manifestations of romantic love with its fantasies and its mores, as well as for the complex social structure that has grown out of our concept of the "family unit." There has been the consummation of the instinctive drive for the perpetuation of the species, the joy and fulfillment of which has produced in the fertile mind of man the sense of romantic love, which in turn produced a sense of possessiveness upon which we have based our entire social structure. It is not difficult to understand how Sigmund Freud went so far in his rationalization that at the basis of all, there is to be found the imprint of sex, sexuality, and sexual relationships.

We have borne a burden of not knowing in the area

of sex unlike any other. For a part of human experience so vital and so instinctive, it is difficult to understand that we have, at least during the past five hundred years, created a system of morality that has caused us to be almost unable to discuss or communicate our understanding to those in our charge. It would seem that during the period of recorded history we have relegated to men, as distinct from women, the responsibility for and authority about sex. But neither men nor women seem to have any more than an instinct for sex . . . certainly no knowledge or appreciation of it except what is learned by experience. In virtually all other areas of physical expression it is considered appropriate to school our children, but not in sex. We work diligently and discuss extensively methods for toilet training and table manners. We teach those coming after us to write and dance and speak and manipulate, yet in Victorian times it was considered totally inappropriate even for a husband and wife to use the word *sex,* let alone to discuss sex in any way. For centuries, we learned about sex and sexual relationships from our peers, who were just as ignorant as we were. Surely a part of the light and wisdom of our time involves a recognition of the importance of growing out of not knowing about this fundamental part of our human experience. Too, it is a part of the light and wisdom of our time to come into the realization that this part of our human experience is also very much a part of our spiritual experience.

The need to touch, and in touching to be stimulated in a unifying relationship; the need to be touched, and in being touched to be stimulated in drawing closer to the toucher, is as basic as any need that mankind has. From our earliest experience we are subject to and strengthened by the gentle touch of parental love. Psychologists have agreed that physical contact is a basic requirement of humanity. The child that is denied this basic, normal expression will be a maladjusted, destructive, and self-destructive personality. The child that from the beginning of his life experience receives the outward, physical expression of love stands an infinitely better chance of maturing in a constructive and productive way. To suggest that this parent-child relationship of touching is a part of sex is a disturbing thought to many. It is disturbing to the extent that we continue to believe that sex in and of itself is evil or sinful or inappropriate. It is disturbing so long as we do not understand the primary purpose and real value of sex. Sex as a part of the love relationship that embraces every level of our human expression, not just the physical, is the means by which we can and shall come into an awareness of the truth of our inseparable unity with every other soul. Our mating experiences surely are not limited to coition.

As we have seen, we mate spiritually, we mate emotionally, we mate mentally or intellectually, and we mate in many ways and on many levels physically. All of the unifying activity of our growth from not knowing into conscious, willed, and willful Self-consciousness is accomplished in some expression of mating. We put our God away from us at a point in our evolution, in a separateness of spirituality as distinct from materiality. Is it not conceivable that sex in its broadest sense is a vital part of the process of awakening to and being established in unity? The transitive verb *to mate* is defined as "to couple or associate as mate or equal." We have not understood the significance of the last word in this definition, and as a result we have given greater significance to man over woman and to God over man. Once we understand that there is but one Presence and one Power in the universe, God, the good omnipotent, and that we are that Presence and Power, we will perceive the foolishness of separating God or one another. In Truth, man is not greater than woman and woman is not greater than man. In Truth, God is not greater than man and man is not greater than God. There is one Presence, one Allness; there is no separation in Truth, there is only God, for all is God and God is all.

The many levels of physical expression of our love relationships must be seen to be equally important, equally unimportant; not good or bad, but simply part of a process directed toward unity. When as an infant we perceive, though perhaps without understanding, our love relationship with our mother or father or brothers or sisters, or with any or all of these collectively, we have begun once more the mating process that moves us toward unity. When we hesitantly share a toy with another child, we are involved in the mating process. When we feel threatened by the beauty, prowess, or popularity of a peer and we experience the sense of separation that our inadequacy or inferiority seems to demand, we are in the process of developing the need to possess that which is beautiful, powerful, or popular. We begin early to lay claim to others, either in fantasy or in fact. In order that we may be secure in that possession and that it may be fulfilling and satisfying to us, we seek acceptable and appropriate ways of giving physical expression to that relationship. For the boy (who is supposed, as a result of our not knowing, to be the dominant one of the couple) to muster the courage to touch or caress is infinitely more of a challenge than most adults seem capable of remembering. There was a beautiful sequence in a motion picture in which the teenage lad struggles painfully to get his arm around his date in the movies. Any man or woman with any sensitivity had no difficulty in relating to the boy and his apparent inadequacy in dealing with not only his basic drive or need, but with the restricting pressures of a society burdened with not knowing.

Falling in love is the direct result of our readiness to grow out of separateness. There is that indefinable, indescribable feeling of need to possess and be possessed by the object of our love. It is an emotion, a feeling, a sense, an awareness that demands physical expression in some form. It is inextricably a part of our instinct toward the preservation and continuation of our species. It is an emotional, mental, and physical demand for oneness. By falling in love, we begin the process of becoming one with the other. We become one in thought and interest and feeling, and ultimately, through many stages of expression, we become one physically with the other. We give and receive the gift of an intimate touch, a caress, a fondling. We experience the surge of physical need that results in the rise of passion. At first, because of our not knowing, this can be a frightening experience, but as we gain control through increased knowing and familiarity through experience, we come to know this to be one of the most beautiful experiences of our human life. The great tragedy of our not knowing in the area of sex is that we have clothed the entire experience in the garb of iniquity. We have, because of our not knowing, made this love experience dirty and base, when in reality it is the most complete act of the unifying process that we have yet discovered. Those who have caused us to feel repulsed by the need for and the act of sex have done so because in our not knowing we have not understood the breadth of the experience that is available to us. We have seen it only as a physical act, one that demeans one or both partners. We have, because of our not knowing, used the power of sex, its availability or denial, as a limiting power of possession over another. We have developed certain standards by which sex can be considered acceptable, and even then there are those of us who seem incapable of beholding any goodness whatsoever in the act, its contemplation or consideration.

The sex act should be seen to be the culmination of the mating process that is the result of our having mated emotionally, in our feeling nature, and mentally or intellectually, in our thought process. In the unity we share on these less intimate or personal levels there is the basis for dignifying the physical act of coition and the foreplay that is so important to its successful completion. We are not animals who are driven blindly to copulate; we are or can be sensitive spiritual beings who share the self that we are with the self of the one whom we love. In this sharing can be and should be the highest form of uniting. There is no portion or form of this most personal and intimate relationship that is either good or bad. Whatever is considerate of each, ennobling and uplifting of each, is surely appropriate. Both the man and the woman who share in a physical love relationship should give and be given the freedom of expression that allows each to give more than is required and to receive more than is deserved. Because of our not knowing, and because of the mystery in which we have allowed this relationship to be shrouded, there is little readily-available, communicable knowledge by which to find and give fulfillment. In recent years there have been published some fine texts on sexual relationships, and there has been produced an awful lot of trash that is more prurient than informational. A careful and prayerful search can make available some good information for those who seek greater fulfillment in their sexual relationships. Still, the greatest "teacher" is the thoughtful, considerate exploration that is mutually shared and lovingly and tactfully discussed by both parties. If each partner in the relationship seeks primarily to provide the greatest fulfillment and satisfaction to the other, increasing joy as well as freeing maturity will result.

In its highest expression, a love relationship that is equally experienced and manifested emotionally, mentally, and physically is the immediate forerunner to true human mating that makes of us and our experience a truly spiritual force. In the maturity of this love experience we can be a vital force in the dissolution of all sense of separation, and thereby achieve greater unity with God through our greater unity with humankind. There is a sacredness in the joy and fulfillment that comes of true mating that makes us ever more one in every way with our God, the one Presence and one Power. It is not difficult to understand the importance we have given to sex. In our not knowing, we have sensed its significance even though we have been limited in our expression or understanding of it. Down through the centuries, sex has had an ever recurring involvement (in one way or another) in our religious observances or experiences. In all of the living religions of the world, there have been those sects that incorporated the sex act or rejection of the sex act as a basic part of their worship. To this day, in remote areas of thought and understanding within the recognized religions of the world, there are those who participate in sexual orgies in the name of religion. There are also many who take the vow of chastity as a part of their spiritual worship.

As we see this part of our wonderful God-given, God-endowed life experience as simply a part of the allness and onliness of God, we can free ourself from darkness and the sense of sinful iniquity. How wonderful it would be if each soul were drawn into this life experience through a continuing act of beautiful, sensitive, generous, and fulfilling union, bathed in the light of our knowing our true Self-consciousness.

CHAPTER XI

We grow in our true Self-consciousness as we continue to develop effective means of communication. In the earliest dawnings of our consciousness of deity, we recognized the need for communicating with deity in ways that would prove effective in our expanding relationship with deity. In our not knowing, we have developed skills in cajoling God, in bargaining with God, in begging and beseeching God, and in bribing Him with all sorts of sacrifices, gifts, and tithes. Prayer has been, in one form or another, a vitally important part of our faltering attempts to communicate with God.

In the broadest sense prayer can be seen to include a vast variety of activities of man. Plant, animal, and monetary sacrifices were surely attempts on the part of man to pray, to communicate, and in doing so to obtain a desired goal. Worship in the formal sense— psalms, hymns, dances, and incantations—was part of mankind's attempts to communicate with deity. It is not difficult to trace the evolution of these attempts at communication from almost bestial sacrifice to meditation. For our purposes here, we will deal with the general forms of communication that can be readily defined as prayer. The mass, the liturgical forms that have become considerably more than just custom within many areas of Christianity, are in the broadest sense modes of communication with God. For most participants, however, such ritualistic forms cannot be considered objectively, because they are inseparably a part of the church. The church has taken on a personality of its own, and to the degree that it has, it tends to fail in the purpose for which it was orginally created.

Originally the church was simply the congregation—those who had been drawn together in order to experience mutually the presence of God. Christianity was originally (and should be now) the embracing of the Truth that was brought and taught by Jesus, the Christ. Today, Christianity to a very marked degree has become "churchianity." That is, the primary emphasis seems to be on the development and maintenance of systems of worship for their own sake rather than for what they cause to occur in those involved. Much of the dogma of denominational Christianity is aimed at the perpetuation of the church, not in its idealistic sense, but in its physical and organizational sense. The church, like all the other institutions that man has formed out of his not knowing and his constant striving toward spiritual Self-consciousness, is neither good nor bad, and in reality does not have identity of its own. We have come to reverence the church as a thing in and of itself, but the only reality the church has is the reality that we continue to give it in our consciousness of not knowing. Surely a part of the light of our age is the insight that will not take away any of the intrinsic value of the church but rather will allow us to make of our home and our business, our field and our factory, no less a place of worship.

As we have seen, many of the forms of communication that we have devised either have become extinct or are so crystallized in ritualistic forms that they no longer serve the purpose for which they have been devised. Prayer alone maintains enough in the way of malleability that we can utilize it intelligently through modification and experience some real, God-directed communication. Doing so, we can make some real progress in our growth process toward spiritual Self-consciousness. Let us look at prayer traditionally and then ideally, and let us see what we have in the way of a handle that we can grasp to move forward in our application of true communication.

Traditionally, prayer has been a process of thought, words, and physical positioning by which we might get God to do something that He is not already doing, or be something that He is not already being. We have believed traditionally that if we thought Godward in a sincere enough way, in a pious enough way, in an honest enough way, or in a convincing enough way, we might get God's attention sufficiently to persuade Him in His loving nature to help us out of our difficulties. "Oh, dear God, in Your infinite mercy hear our plea; behold our ailing loved one and call forth the power of Your healing presence to free him from his disease and pain." "If You are there, God, please touch the life of my innocent child in this time of challenge." Once (a good many years ago now) I crouched in a foxhole and thought thoughts of prayer. Perhaps if I had verbalized my thoughts they would have sounded something like this: "Father, I am frightened and I desperately seek Your protecting presence. Gather around me Your heavenly host that will keep this evil enemy I am facing from hurting me. Please, in Your wisdom make each of my shots reach their mark and thus help me play my part in bringing this madness of war to an end. Thank You, Father, that You hear me, for I know that You do. Amen." As I looked over the edge of the hole that was for me a protective hiding place, I saw one of the enemy, across the snow-covered field ahead of me, jump out of his protective hiding place, drop to his knees, and cross himself in the fashion of Roman Catholics. I am sure that not only was he performing a ritualistic act of prayer, but that there were thoughts of prayer going through his mind too. If he verbalized his thoughts, probably they would not have been a great deal different from my own. The thought went through my mind and has remained with me ever since, that if indeed there is a God and He was watching and listening, He must have thought us very naive. Each of us was praying to the same God for the same purpose, only in opposite directions. What must our anthropomorphic God think of us?

If by begging or beseeching, by sincerity or eloquence, by smooth talking we could possibly change God, God must be a pretty inconsistent Being. If on the other hand God is as we have postulated— the one Presence and one Power, absolute principle— then all our words are in vain. All of the eloquence, the smooth talking, the crossing ourself or kneeling in His presence, are for nought. If this naive concept of prayer is what prayer is, then we have no alternative but to assume that it doesn't work. If the purpose, as seems to be rather generally believed, is to change God, then prayer is worthless, for God, if in fact He is infinite and absolute, everywhere equally present within and throughout the universe, cannot be changed by man's not knowing. If prayer is not what so many human beings have believed, what is it?

Prayer certainly is a mind and emotion conditioner. There is tremendous value in prayer as such. Those of us who have been brought up in the Judeo-Christian tradition can be temporarily blessed and strengthened by prayer as a mental and emotional conditioner. To each one who has been exposed to a formal tradition of religion, there are words and phrases, attitudes of thought, feeling, and bodily stance, that have significance. We may not be able to explain logically what happens when we speak or hear those words, or are stirred by those feelings, or take up those physical stances. But obviously we find strength and peace and blessing through them, or we would not go on attending services where they are practiced or spoken, and we would no longer almost instinctively give lip service to them. Traditionally prayer has been and continues to be of value to us in our not knowing. It is of course neither good nor bad; it is simply a process of our limited consciousness that we can and will grow out of.

Prayer is an action of mind and emotion by which we can and do change our own consciousness. By doing so, we bring ourself into harmony with our ever-increasing understanding of God as the one Presence and one Power that is now, always has been, and always will be the Source of all that we can desire. Prayer is not some words, not even some certain feelings; it is not a "thing" that can be observed in the outer by the tilt of the head or the closed eyes and folded hands that have, in our not knowing,

91

become synonymous with it. Prayer is a conditioned state of readiness, it is an affirmation, and it is a receptivity. Prayer is a communication, but as we shall come to see and understand, it is far more a receiving activity than a transmitting one. Perhaps a big and important part of our growth as the result of the light for our age is that of understanding this most important part of true spiritual communication.

Prayer is a conditioned state of readiness. All of the physical talents that we develop in this life experience are brought to a degree of excellence or proficiency by virtue of discipline and practice. The dictionary defines discipline as "training which corrects, molds, strengthens, or perfects." A disciple is "one who receives instruction from another . . . an adherent of a school, as in art or philosophy." The conditioned state of readiness that is such an important part of prayer can readily be realized through some discipline that has significance to us. Traditional liturgical forms of worship that have through usage assured a conditioned response of peace or poise or quietude can be valuable to our prayer experience. It is not necessary to abandon those forms that have been meaningful to us, as long as we can, in the light of increased understanding, utilize them to our benefit. The Eastern mystic who assumes the lotus position for meditation, or the modern traditional Christian who recites the Lord's Prayer or the Twenty-third Psalm, can be moving into a conditioned state of readiness. If we mistakenly assume that the position, the tranquillity of the mind, or the recitation of those words that have significance to us, are enough, we shall probably go on being burdened with the doubts about the efficacy of prayer that are so common among us today.

Our conditioned state of readiness requires us to be free of concern or caring about that condition in life that has caused us to pray. In other words, there is no place in true prayer for a consciousness of or a recitation of our problems. Right here is where most of us, in our not knowing, have our greatest difficulty. Without having given it any constructive, creative, or original thought, we assume that we should take our cares, our problems, our needs into prayer. This is not so, for the conditions or things or persons about which we would pray are nothing. They do not deserve the attention of our thought, for our thought is a creative force that is God. Again we must remind ourself that there is only one Presence and one Power in the universe, God, the good omnipotent, and that we are that force seeking expression and manifestation. We are not poor, miserable creatures who are beset with a burden of disease or pain or lack. We don't have to overcome the conditions that are undesirable in our world; we are God, seeking through ourself an ever-increasing state of accuracy and perfection.

There is a whole new area of research, known as "biofeedback training," which utilizes electronic equipment that measures the degree of readiness that our discipline calls forth. Dr. Elmer Green of the Menninger Clinic has been an inspired pioneer in the development of this simple technique. Bodily temperature changes and recognizable brain waves can be measured by this equipment and thus assist us in knowing when we have arrived at that state of conditioned readiness. Certain exercises and breathing techniques that are a part of yoga training for many are helpful in moving into such a state. Any of these techniques or methods can be valuable. Simply sitting comfortably in a quiet, comfortable place, free from disturbance or interference by outside sounds or movement or light, and speaking words that will quiet and center us in ready realization of the omnipresence of God that we are, will suffice.

The effectiveness of this important phase of prayer is directly attributable to the amount of discipline we bring to bear through practice. It is important for the conscious student of Truth to set aside time every day for disciplined practice of this process that is effectual prayer. If one wishes to be a concert pianist, one must discipline himself sufficiently in daily practice so that it becomes natural to strike the right notes in the right sequence with the right feeling or interpretation. One who operates a bookkeeping machine or a computer or a lathe or a sewing machine must discipline himself, through practice, to a point at which his talent becomes natural. The one who would become proficient in prayer, who would become a communicator with infinite Mind and thus an intentional, willed, and willful expresser of infinite Mind, must discipline himself. He must practice the presence of God which he is. Many people, struggling in not knowing, have cast prayer aside as a useless, naive superstition that doesn't come to grips with the problems of today. You can almost hear their thinking: "Oh, I tried prayer, and it didn't work for me." Such expressions are often sincerely presented, because in our not knowing, we have mistakenly assumed that it was the doing that got the results. It is *coming to be* that gets results, as we shall see.

Affirmation is a tremendous part of the prayer

process that draws man into an active, productive consciousness of himself as an expression of the allness and the oneness that God is. Simply, affirmation is "confirmation . . . ratification . . . assertion . . . an averment." The word *affirm* comes from the Latin and means "to make firm." As we use the word *affirmation,* it is more than a confirmation or ratification; it is the assertion of Truth, it is a state of consciousness, and it is also an action of mind. It is the modern expression of the logos. Charles Fillmore points out in his book *Jesus Christ Heals:* "In Hebrews it is written, 'By faith we understand that the worlds have been framed by the word of God.' In the first chapter of John the Word or Logos is given as the source of all things, and this Word is said to become flesh and be glorified as the only-begotten from the Father. . . . Jesus said that every man would be justified or condemned by his word. He demonstrated the power of the word of faith in His mastery of natural laws and in His many marvelous healings." Affirmation is the activity of the logos, the Word of God, that through which God *said,* "Let there be light." Affirmation is an activity of creative mind in you and me by which we can speak our increasing understanding of God, the one Presence and one Power, into our life, thus releasing the activity of His greater good, His greater power or love or light, into expression and manifestation in our life here and now. Once man was able, as a result of seeing and understanding the principles of aerodynamics, to say, "I can fly," it was simply a matter of the time it took to apply the principles involved before he was able to do so.

Charles Fillmore and many of his contemporaries were ahead of their times in their recognition of the significance of the power of affirmation. Throughout his writings Mr. Fillmore encourages his readers to speak the word of Truth to the extent that they have grasped that Truth. His reason for doing so is profoundly simple and simply profound. In his book *Mysteries of John* Mr. Fillmore says: "The Divine Mind creates under law, that is, spiritual law. Man may get a comprehension of the creative process of Being by analyzing the action of his own mind. First is mind, then the idea in mind of what the act is to be, then the act itself. Thus the Word and the divine process of creating are identical." In true prayer, we acknowledge God-Mind in the peace, poise, and serenity which is that conditioned state of readiness, and in expectation we speak the word.

We affirm the highest conception of good of which we are capable by declaring its reality in mind, with the understanding that in doing so we are going to call forth into expression and manifestation its material, human, or physical counterpart. We practice affirmation by conceiving in words, images, thoughts, and feelings the highest, best, strongest, wisest, and most fulfilling good that we are capable of. We put that ideal into expression as a creative energy, with the expectation that we shall see and experience a similar result. Affirmation is then the attaining and maintaining of a state of consciousness of expectation built around an ideal. It is a positive, constructive assertion of a good that we strive for. Our responsibility is to attain the highest and best concept of the good we aspire to, and then to loose it into the care and keeping of the divine law with which we are working.

This concept can be put in traditional words of

prayer by saying in effect: "This, Father, is my highest concept of the healing or blessing for which I pray, and this is what I seek and accept and affirm. This, Father, or Your greater good!" "I am now one with the love and understanding and peace of infinite mind that is manifesting as order and harmony in my home and family." "The perfect vitality and health of Spirit is now manifest in my mind and body." "God is the instant, constant, and abundant supply of all good in my life now." We affirm these truths and then we release them into the wise and loving activity of Spirit, divine law that is immutable and now at work within and throughout the universe just as surely as it was in the creation of the ideal realm in the mind of God.

In this conceptual part of prayer it is important to see the value of both conceiving of the good for which we pray and releasing that conception "into the hands of the Father." You see, it is difficult not to revert to our approach to God as an anthropomorphic being. Here we have given "Him" hands into which we can place our dream. Nevertheless, doing so can remind us of the importance of releasing that for which or about which we pray. Your consciousness and mine need the exercise, the practice that comes of visualizing the good for which we pray.

Many Truth students use a clever technique called treasure mapping. One cuts out of magazines those words or phrases or pictures that depict the good for which he prays. These are pasted on a large cardboard, which is hung in a conspicuous place where it will be seen every day. This visualizing technique has proved to be remarkably effective for many people who use it. Other students use a variation of the technique in writing out statements of Truth that depict the good for which they pray, and these are taped up on the bathroom mirror or on the window over the sink or under the glass on the desk. The visualization process is important, because it is necessary for our consciousness to begin to grow into an awareness of the greater good toward which we strive. Until our consciousness does expand, the good will be denied us—not by God or fate, but by the very limitations of our consciousness that we have imposed in our not knowing.

It is necessary for us to develop our highest concept of the good for which we pray, but we must not limit ourself to that concept. It is in the letting go that this conceptual part of prayer allows the greater wisdom, the greater good to flow forth. When meeting in consciousness His greatest overcoming, Jesus is recorded as having said: "My Father, if it be possible, let this cup pass from me; nevertheless, not as I will, but as thou wilt." Jesus Christ knew the Father-God to be all-wise, all-knowing, and He expressed His faith in that knowing by releasing Himself and His life. We may not be confronted with what to human thinking is such a tremendous challenge, but the principle that needs to be applied is just as applicable to our need. We must in all prayer experience provide the addendum, "not as I will, but as thou wilt."

We must provide a conditioned state of readiness; we must speak the word of the Truth that we would manifest; we must then release the idea, the need and its outworking, into the care and keeping of the activity of divine principle; then there is something else that we must do. We must receive in consciousness that for which and about which we have prayed.

Meditation is the receiving part of effectual prayer. It must be understood that we are still in prayer, and are not yet concerned with the expression or manifestation of that for which or about which we pray. Think back to the important idea that Charles Fillmore shared in observing that first there had to be the idea, then the idea in mind, and then its manifestation. We must through the effective use of meditation get the idea established in mind, and we must draw to conscious awareness all that is needful in the way of understanding for the eventual expression and manifestation of the good for which we pray.

Most people fail to understand that not only in intentional prayer but all the time, day and night, we are responsible for the direction of mind energy. Mind energy is no less an energy than are muscle power, electrical power, or atomic power. In reality, it is infinitely more than any of these lesser expressions of energy. Do you see what we are considering here? We are suggesting that mind energy, yours or mine, is greater in potential than any energy that we have conceived of or harnessed to date! You have, right now, access to control of an energy more powerful than that released in an atomic explosion! "Greater than the tread of mighty armies is an idea whose hour has come." This is true because an idea comes into expression by virtue of mind energy. The mind energy that we utilize within the boundaries of our not knowing may seem limited or even paltry, but it is still mind energy that is without limitation. We use mind energy—or better still, we *are* mind energy, expressing itself as us or through us and our consciousness according to our awareness of it. Once we tear away the limitations of not knowing, we shall recognize this energy that lies dormant within our thought process.

Meditation is the vehicle by which we come into control of mind energy and direct it toward the accomplishment of the goals that we set for ourself through the power of affirmation. Many human beings, because of not knowing, utilize the power of affirmation to make firm in consciousness those very conditions that they abhor; then the tremendous power that is mind energy goes to work to bring into expression and manifestation the substance and life and power of God in the form of that which they fear or hate. Job recognized the potency of this divine law working to his detriment when he said, "For the thing that I fear comes upon me, and what I dread befalls me." If the law works to our detriment (and we can see evidences of it on every hand), it will work for us also in a positive and constructive sense.

As a part of our prayer discipline every day, there should be times set aside during which we meditate. One of the greatest stumbling blocks in the way of effective meditation is the mistaken assumption that one should stop thinking, or think about nothing, in meditation. But that is not possible. The mind is a mass of energy and ideas, and it is its nature to move either in directions given it or down the habitual lines of least resistance. If it is our habit to fret and worry and stew about the negative and limiting circumstances of our life experience, our thought process will automatically turn in this direction unless it is otherwise directed. If we have disciplined ourself, or will discipline ourself to be conscious of the one Presence and Power that God is in the very midst of us and all around us, in meditative practice the mind will automatically turn Godward.

In meditation we should choose a time and place where we will have the least likelihood of being disturbed, where there is a minimum of noise or light to distract us, and where we can be as comfortable as possible. The body can be a great source of distraction if our thought has to keep returning to it to respond to discomfort or pain or stress. We should develop techniques by which we can put aside our harried thoughts of concern for the conditions in life that are demanding our attention.

Through the power of thought, open an imaginary container on the floor beside you and place in it each of the pressures, each of the concerns, each of the problems in your life. Do so with the understanding that when you have finished your time of meditation, you can open the container again and find each of your problems safe and undisturbed. You can, if you choose to, pick them up again and carry on with your concern about them. Once you have placed all of your problems in the container on the floor, take another imaginary container and place it on your lap. Let this one, (through the power of your creative imagination), be the one in which you keep the precious dreams toward which you are working. Perhaps in this container you will place the dream of the loving and harmonious relationship that you are working toward with your husband or wife or child or neighbor. With your imagination, you can hold that dream for a long enough period of time that the infinite Mind of which yours is but an expression can continue to reveal to you the sense of its existence as a reality now.

Eastern philosophies recommend the visualization

of bright light and the repetition of a tone, or a mantra. The mantra can be a series of words that represent for you the allness and onliness of the Spirit in which you dwell. If the opportunity for such training in discipline is available to you, it may be of tremendous value.

Many of us fail to understand that even though we are eager to experience that for which we pray, even desperate about it, we are not yet receptive to the good or we would have it. The purpose of meditation is to develop a consciousness of receptivity to the good that God is, and the portion of the divine goodness that we have so far conceived. The importance of regular, disciplined meditation cannot be overemphasized. A child who is given the opportunity to take piano lessons finds it difficult to understand the importance of daily practice. The child in us often has the difficulty in understanding the importance of daily meditation. Sometimes it is not easy to discern the progress we are making as a result of the daily discipline, and it becomes easy to rationalize the importance of other things that need to be done by us.

In considering meditation, we must realize that our consciousness is not only filled with not knowing from eons of time, but it is constantly being subjected to tremendous pressures of negative thought. Newspapers are filled with graphic reports of violence on every hand. Television dramatically and artistically portrays all the fear and hatred to be found on the surface of the consciousness of our civilization. In order to give that portrayal the greatest amount of viewer appeal, the "reality" of ugliness is portrayed in living (and dying) color. The majority of idle conversation seem to be directed to the support and maintenance of negativity.

An acquaintance passes you on the street and says: "Good morning! How are you today?" If you are not a disciplined individual, you may tell him. In reality, he is not seeking a physiological evaluation or a financial report or a marital-status bulletin; he is simply trying to be courteous and friendly. We get caught up in this kind of experience and we not only listen to the "organ recital" of our ailing friend, but we find ourself seeing if we can outdo him in his misfortune.

Even though the conscious part of our mind is eager to attain growth and overcoming, there is a part of us that does find satisfaction and fulfillment in the nature or degree of our discomfort. It is difficult for us to appreciate the subtle power of guilt, frustration, and self-recrimination that may be at the bottom of our suffering. After all, it must be remembered that the limitations we experience did not come to us by virtue of some power or force outside of ourself. We are the artificer of our soul and of our life.

We must be alert to the deduction we have made here. We are stating that the conditions or circumstances out of which we are struggling are of our own making. This is not an easy thought to embrace. After all, we probably have an elaborate rationalization that lays the blame for what we experience at another's feet. It is the fault of our parents, our education or lack of it, the race into which we were born, not having been born with any kind of spoon in our mouth (let alone a silver one), or the government, the system. Not knowing that we are in a position of dominion and authority, whether we have understood this or not, we have created all sorts of obstacles in the way of productive meditation. As a result we have not been really receptive to the good for which we have begged and prayed and cried. A consciousness of receptivity not only must be developed, it *can* be developed here and now.

Whether or not you feel that you understand how meditation can create a consciousness of receptivity through which your mind energy can mold and fashion a new world for you, set aside time each day, several times a day, and begin the practice of meditation. You may want to work at it for brief periods of time at first, and then gradually extend the time period until you can experience this time of peace and poise and receptivity for ten or fifteen minutes at a sitting. Many persons find that it is best to have specific times each day so that a constructive habit can be developed. Remember, prayer is a conditioned state of readiness, it is an affirmation, and it is a receptivity . . . and you bear responsibility for it.

CHAPTER XII

In all sincerity (and based upon a tremendous amount of knowledge of disease, the body's susceptibility and its recuperative powers) the medical doctor diagnoses a condition and offers his prognosis: "Particulates of calcium have begun to build up here between these abutting bones, and it is this buildup that has caused the sharp pain each time you raise your arm. You will just have to learn to live with it; it won't get better, it will probably continue to build up and cause you considerable pain from time to time." From his knowledge of disease, that is probably a reasonably accurate diagnosis and prognosis of the condition. The doctor, who has learned all about disease, makes his judgment based upon that knowledge. Unfortunately, if he is an average doctor, he has not had the opportunity to learn much about the nature of health. While from his standpoint the diagnosis is accurate, it does not take into consideration the tremendous truth that lies behind man's not knowing about the divinity of the body. "Do you not know that your body is a temple of the Holy Spirit within you, which you have from God? You are not your own."

A medical officer cleaned quite a number of small shrapnel wounds in a soldier's legs. He prodded a bit and then he sprinkled sulfa powder on the wounds and bandaged the larger ones. When the officer excused the soldier to return to duty, the soldier asked, "Aren't you going to take the bits of steel out?" The doctor assured him that this wouldn't be necessary. The soldier comforted himself (with a healthy sense of humor) by wondering what it would be like to walk down the street in years to come, clanking a bit. Of course he didn't clank at all, because in a few months each of those tiny bits of steel worked its way to the surface of his body. The body has a most remarkable ability to protect itself from foreign objects by enfolding them in a sort of gristle and then easing them out toward the surface of the body, there allowing them to drop off or be rubbed off.

In not knowing about the divinity of our body, in not knowing that the substance out of which it is made is perfect, eternal, and pure, in not knowing that our mind and our feelings have a great deal to do with what happens in and to our body, we have created all sorts of limitations that need to be outgrown. The eternal soul that you are or I am has, according to its awareness of Truth, drawn together the substance and energy that have formed the body temple. We who are housed in this body have the responsibility and the authority to cause the building process of life in us to continue to perfect, strengthen, and heal the body. Though in our not knowing we may have suffered limitations in and about the body, the soul that we are can and must seek an ever-expanding awareness of the Truth about ourself and move forward to experience healing.

The need for healing is to be seen on every hand.

Great sciences have been developed in an attempt to assist us in the fulfilling of our responsibility to heal. Though these sciences have grown out of our not knowing, they still are a vitally important part of the development of our knowing. We must be grateful for the tremendous strides that have been made in the healing arts and in the sciences that have produced such wonderful technology for the easing of physical suffering.

There have been those who, in the search for Truth, have rejected medicine, doctors, curative techniques, and treatments on the physical level. It is a laudable demonstration of faith that causes sincere seekers after Truth to take this step, but it is done so out of a consciousness of not knowing. It is important for us to remember that there is one Presence and one Power in the universe, God, the good omnipotent. A part of that one Presence and one Power is the chemical that aids in the adjustment of our bodily balance, the surgical skill and knowledge that have been developed by one whose life is dedicated to healing, and the knowledge of nutrition that directs us to feed and nourish our body properly and adequately.

If you or anyone you know is suffering any form of disease of the mind or body, rejoice and give thanks that it is so. Don't rejoice and give thanks for sickness of pain or physical limitation, but give thanks that you are aware of a need to grow in your consciousness of physical and mental well-being. Whenever there is pain in your body or mind, it is because the mental energy that flows from your mind into every cell, organ, and function of your body is momentarily deterred in its perfect purpose.

Pain is the signal that calls to our attention the need for adjustment. If we in our not knowing ignore this divine signal, we cause the mind energy to build obstructions to its natural and harmonious function. Such obstructions are given frightening names, and as we behold in others the debilitating effects of the obstructions, we add to their strength by our fear and not knowing. Could we not at this point in our evolving understanding come to recognize that our wonderful, beautiful, intelligent body is working twenty-four hours a day, seven days a week, to manifest the most nearly perfect balance of physical well-being that it can, according to the degree of knowledge of the Truth we have given it? The body is not an evil thing, iniquitous and subject to everlasting pain and suffering, destined to end up in pain and agony and death. The body is the perfect outpicturing of our consciousness of ourself as God expressing Himself as us at this moment.

Right now we can alter our consciousness of health and well-being. Right now we can bring strength and vitality where there has been weakness and lassitude. Right now we can call back into expression the wisdom that partakes of good food to manifest the energy and vitality required to be and do all the things that need to be done by us. You can be healed, regardless of the prognosis you may have been given by the world of materiality and its judgments. Do you believe it? If not, give some thought to the logic of what we are beholding in the perception of this new light, this new wisdom for our age. If it is true that we are the one Presence and Power, and if it is true that that one Presence and one Power is good, then there must be a way in which we can overcome the conditions that have been manifest as a result of our not knowing. Perhaps the first thing we should do is become aware of the fact that in a sense, many of us experience disease because a part of us wants to, and we derive a sort of enjoyment from the suffering. This suggestion can be disturbing to many people, because our conscious self would certainly never choose to be ill. Nonetheless, we all from time to time draw experiences to us out of a sense of self-pity, a need for the attention of our loved ones. Haven't you at some time feigned a degree of pain or suffering in order to gain the recognition and attention of a loved one? George Bernard Shaw said: "I enjoy convalescence. It is the part that makes the illness worthwhile."

Psychologists and psychiatrists are convinced that much of the illness we are subject to, both mental and physical, is the direct result of unconscious feelings of guilt. Many of us punish ourself for real or fancied transgressions by conjuring up pain and suffering. The fact that we are capable of doing this can be seen in the degrees of control that Eastern mystics have developed over the normal functioning of their bodies. The fakir can cause the blood to be withheld from a certain portion of his body, or turn off the sense of feeling in a specified area of the body. Most of us have not developed this kind of ability, nor would we particularly wish to do so, but we have the ability to do so. We do it in subtle ways that produce suffering and disease because of our consciousness of not knowing the truth about ourself.

We can experience the healing activity of God in a simple and wonderful way. We have acknowledged that there is tremendous mind energy available to us, and we have seen that a blockage of that mind energy in our body can and does cause pain and suffering. By accepting our dominion and authority over our body temple and the conscious, willed direction of the infinite mind energy that is available to us, we can alter any condition that we may experience. Of the thirty-five miracles attributed to Jesus Christ, twenty-six of them were miracles of healing. The followers of Jesus marveled at these miracles and He said to them, "Truly, truly, I say to you, he who believes in me will also do the works that I do; and greater works than these will he do . . . " We have Scriptural authority for our belief in our dominion and authority, both in the story of creation and in the life and teachings of Jesus Christ. We also have ample evidence from disciples other than our own that man can attain ever greater and greater control over his body simply by controlling his mind. Modern science, through the study and treatment of the whole man, has begun to prove the power of the mind that is available to everyone. The light or wisdom that is new in our age is the determination to accept the power and authority that is ours by virtue of our newly recognized divinity.

When you become aware of a need for healing in your body or that of a loved one, begin by rejoicing in the recognition of that condition. Be grateful that you are aware enough to claim dominion and authority for another. When you are working for another's healing, what you are really seeking to do is experience the healing of your awareness of that person's need for healing. The responsibility for healing rests with the soul that experiences the need for healing. We can sustain and strengthen a loved one in our healing consciousness and we can heal our consciousness of his need, but the responsibility is his to direct the mind energy that will draw together the substance and life that will manifest as health and well-being. We must first be moved with a spirit of joy and gratitude, a consciousness of faith and expectancy. It may take some time and prayerful discipline to come to this consciousness of expectancy, but it is important and must be attained.

Lay hold of the idea that you do have dominion and authority, and that you can experience the healing you seek. Move in thought toward the conditioned state of readiness that expects the results for which you work. Know with your mind and feel with your deep feeling nature that you are centered and poised in the allness and onliness of infinite Mind. There is only one Presence and one Power in the universe, and you are that Presence and Power. Rest for a time in quiet realization of yourself as the very center of the universe, open and receptive to the flow of mind energy that you can and must control. Visualize the source of the mind energy as just behind your forehead. Sense it as a reality moving down through your body to that point of obstruction. Continue to relax, for tension will only obstruct your direction of the infinite mind energy that is yours. If you feel yourself tensing in your fear of the condition that you are dissolving, take a moment to breathe deeply and relax anew. An effective thought at this point is, "I am poised and centered in the infinite Mind of the Christ that I am; I relax, I let go, and I let God express through me."

Feel with your creative thought the mind energy moving freely and easily through the point of ob-

111

struction, allowing the free flow of Spirit. "See" that point of obstruction in your body and speak inwardly, easily, the word of Truth: "I freely and easily let go of all I no longer need or desire." Now be still. Hold gently to the thought of the activity of Spirit that is at work in you. Sense the peace of Spirit that is embracing the cells and organs and functions with which you are constructively concerned at this moment. Be still . . . be still and know that you are God. Abide now in that meditative spirit which is receptive to the complete and perfect healing you seek, and to the thoughts and ideas that will assist in calling forth the manifestation of the healing.

Let the final part of this prayer treatment be a consciousness of thanksgiving. Rejoice and give thanks for the consciousness of healing that is even now directing the flow of mind energy toward the adjustment of imbalanced parts that together have produced dis-ease. For many it is necessary to repeat this kind of constructive effort, and with each assertion of dominion and authority, each affirmation of Truth, and each time of resting in a consciousness of receptivity, we grow in our awareness of God-self and the expression and manifestation of who and what we are in Truth.

CHAPTER XIII

Much of the life of Jesus is portrayed in the miracles that He performed in the lives of those He served. He caused in the lives of many the manifestation of healing and at that time (and ever since) multitudes walked in His footsteps in search of healing. In our not knowing, we assumed and continue to assume that healing or blessing in any form was the purpose of His ministry. Surely this is not true. The purpose of the life, the teachings, and the ministry of Jesus Christ was and is to make us know that we too can and must attain the same degrees of awareness of unity that He attained. By His own declaration, the purpose of His ministry was to teach us to surpass our mentor.

In the sixth chapter of John we are told: "And a multitude followed him, because they saw the signs which he did on those who were diseased. . . . Lifting up his eyes, then, and seeing that a multitude was coming to him, Jesus said to Philip, 'How are we to buy bread, so that these people may eat?' . . . One of his disciples, Andrew, Simon Peter's brother, said to him, 'There is a lad here who has five barley loaves and two fish; but what are they among so many?' Jesus said, 'Make the people sit down.' Now there was much grass in the place, so the men sat down, in number about five thousand. Jesus then took the loaves, and when he had given thanks, he distributed them to those who were seated; so also the fish, as much as they wanted. And when they had eaten their fill, he told his disciples, 'Gather up the fragments left over, so that nothing may be lost.' So they gathered them up and filled twelve baskets with fragments from the five barley loaves, left by those who had eaten."

This miracle of the feeding of the five thousand is well known to every Christian and has been a cause for hope in many hearts. At the same time, it has been a source of consternation to many people, in their not knowing. By all the laws of nature that we know, it is not possible to feed five thousand people with five little loaves and two small fish . . . let alone have so much left over when all have been fed. In our not knowing we have accepted the limitations of the material world rather than understanding the divine laws of the spiritual world. We have allowed ourself to live in lack and limitation, even though we dwell eternally in a limitless bounty that we have not even begun to conceive.

The concept of infinity, of the unendingness of time and space reaching out without end, is for many people a terrifying and confusing one. Whether or not we have difficulty with this thought, at least we can conceive of all the time and space we can encompass in our thought being filled with substance and energy. Every plant, every creature, the earth itself, the atoms that make up the air and moisture that surround our earth and all of space, the suns and moons and planets that fill that space—all are made up of substance and energy that is indeed infinite. It is everywhere equally present. It is, as we have postulated, like ourself the very presence of God. God is the substance and energy that fills and transcends all time and space. The mind energy that we direct as co-creators with God-Mind is now expressing that infinity according to our finite consciousness. We have brought forth a wonderful bounty of good things, but with that bounty we have brought forth limitation and lack, to which we have given a sense of reality. All around us there is an unending sea of substance and energy that we have direct access to, and according to our understanding and our lack of understanding we are constantly fashioning that malleable mind stuff. God is the instant, constant, and abundant supply of all good, and we are, through our direction of mind energy, the formative artists that make our world.

Let us be quite conscious of what we are accepting here. There is an anthropomorphic deity who is responsible for the bounty of our world, or for the lack and limitation that we experience in it. Other persons or groups of persons are not responsible for what we experience in the way of opulence or limitation. We and we alone are responsible for what we experience, and we alone have access to the power to change the manifestations in our world. That is a tremendous truth, and one that can be rather frightening to us if we continue to dwell in our not knowing. We may think that it would seem easier and nicer if someone or something else could be blamed or acclaimed for our world, but if we are to grow in Self-consciousness, we must come to accept this truth. Though it may be frightening, it can open doors to dominion and authority that we have not yet dreamed of. It takes a lot of courage to be big enough to be God expressing Himself as us, but we can and we will ultimately come to do so. It is our divine heritage, and it must be lived out.

Where you behold lack of any good thing, you must learn to "see" the limitless bounty that God is, filling all time and space. Rejoice in the awareness of the need that has manifested itself, and move forward in consciousness to behold the bounty that God is now. This can be done by using several techniques that have been developed and proved by many seekers after Truth who have gone before us. In the miracle of the feeding of the five thousand, Jesus first recognized the need. Surely we can understand that He was not conscious of any lack, but was aware and made others aware of the need that was at hand. Recognize with joy the need that you find in your life; don't cry in lack and limitation as though these have reality. As a living expression of all that God is, you can approach the need that you have become aware of with courage and confidence. Jesus, aware of His eternal oneness with all that His Father-God is, acknowledged what was available on the human or physical level to meet the need: a lad with five barley loaves and two small fishes. To the people of that time, these were as ordinary as ordinary could be. The most common, the most available substance in form was utilized to work an exciting and staggering miracle. What do you have that is as ordinary as ordinary could be? What have you at this moment that is common and available in the way of substance in form, that might be utilized to bring about the miracle you need? We all have time and energy and talent and substance in the form of the currency of our realm. We may not seem to have enough to meet the need, but then neither did Jesus there on the shores of Galilee. Because of their not knowing, even the disciples of Jesus on that day could not anticipate the wonders they were to behold. In our not knowing, we may find it difficult to anticipate what is about to occur in our human experience.

Jesus then told His disciples to have the hungry ones to sit down. Nomads in their flowing robes always sat to eat, making of their robes a table on which they could place the food. So the hungry ones prepared to receive food . . . they prepared to have their need met. Our problem, in our not knowing, is that we become so conscious of the lack that seems to be represented by our need that we fail to prepare to have the need met. A youngster who wanted a bicycle was instructed by his parents to pray about it. After having done so, he was discovered by his father, busily cleaning out the garage. He explained that he was making a place for his new bicycle. This is the kind of preparation that we must enter into if we would see our need filled. We must prepare ourself in consciousness and in the outer to receive the good for which we pray. What have you done, besides bemoan your lack, to prepare for the manifestation of its fulfillment? More important than that, what can you do to be ready for your good?

Jesus took the loaves, and when He had given thanks He broke the bread and handed it out to the hungry. He did the same with the fish; when they had all eaten and were filled, He had the disciples pick up the remaining pieces so that they would not be wasted. Sharing is the process by which Jesus multiplied the loaves and the fishes, and sharing is the way in which we too can multiply the good in our life. It must be understood that the law of sharing is one that must be constantly applied, not just when we are aware of need in our life. "Give, and it will be given to you; good measure, pressed down, shaken together, running over, will be put into your lap. For the measure you give will be the measure you get back." With the same generosity and freedom that you give, you will receive. This is a divine law that we have failed to comprehend. Because of our not knowing, we have sought to hold and to keep what we believed to be ours. Nothing is ours, and yet all is ours. Nothing is ours to keep, to take out of circulation and hold away from others. All is ours to draw upon to meet any need. We have failed to comprehend that what we keep, we lose, and what we give away in faith is ours eternally.

In recognition of this fundamental truth, the law of tithing was conceived and established as a law of action many centuries ago. The enlightened ones recognized men's need for discipline, in order that they might be in charge of their lives rather than having someone or something else be in charge of them. The law of tithing has been defined as the selection of a prescribed portion of our bounty to be set aside and returned to the Source from which it came. Down through the centuries, this has come to mean that a tenth of our bounty is to be given to God, or to those institutions that exist for the primary purpose of making us aware of His presence and power. The law itself is far more than a formality of exchange by which we support God-directed activity. The law is that all that comes to us, in whatever form, must be kept in circulation. We must come to understand that we are to give of all the forms of God's limitless good that comes into our life, just as the rose gives of its beauty and fragrance constantly. People and organizations that have grasped the significance of this law and what it truly means have proved again and again that man cannot give away faster than God can provide. The successful application of the law requires that we understand the principle involved, and not assume that the physical act of moving formed substance from one place to another will necessarily manifest additional formed substance. Do you see the difference? The principle is applicable on all levels of consciousness, not just in the material realm.

For many, the thought of this kind of commitment is a frightening one. If it is so for you, take it in easy steps. Work first on the idea that God is indeed everywhere, in all that is manifest as well as in all that is not yet manifest. Build that consciousness first. By the time you do so, you will find yourself so enriched that it will be difficult not to respond to the divine command to give, to share. Then set for yourself a discipline of giving one percent, or one tenth of one percent, but do it on a regular basis, and exercise your consciousness in feeling grateful and joyous in the freedom you have found in sharing what you have manifested. Before you know it, you will be a real tither . . . one who cannot stop from sharing, giving in order that an ever-increasing consciousness of God will be made manifest in the world around you. A real tither is indeed a rich, rich man.

As we apply the principle, we will find that after every need we are conscious of has been met, we will be able to gather up a limitless bounty of good that remains. The principle here defined is not in any way limited to materiality. As it is applied, we will see that every phase of our life is enriched, and we will become a light and a blessing to all with whom we come in contact.

CHAPTER XIV

We have given a lot of consideration to the idea that not knowing is the greatest challenge we have to meet. In our not knowing, we have created all sorts of opportunities through which we can grow as we come into a consciousness of knowing the truth about ourself, our relationship to God, and what that means in our personal, human, and physical relationships. Coming into a consciousness of knowing the truth, we are coming to know our self . . . our self as an expression of God. This, as we have defined it, is conscious Self-awareness. There is no condition in our human, mental, emotional, or physical world that is not the direct result of our knowledge of the truth, or our not knowing the truth. Perhaps the important thing that all this tells us is that we are not so much human beings as we are divine beings.

It may be that we are not ready to accept this truth for ourself; if that is the case with you, let go of it. If there is truth in the recognition of this concept, and we will all one day come to know the truth about ourself as God expressing Himself as us, then we don't have to be overly concerned if at this point we have any difficulty in acceptance. The very fact that you are reading these words is evidence that you are on the path, a seeker after Truth. A major part of the difficulty produced by our not knowing is that we have believed that the Truth for which we search is somehow "out there." We have assumed that it is a treasure hidden in the secrets of the ages, known only by those who have somehow been blessed with a direct line to God, or infinite wisdom. There is a spirit that indwells you and me that has access to all the knowing we shall ever require.

As the Truth continues to reveal itself to you and me, we shall continue to come into the realization of our heritage. Whatever forms or traditions we may have accepted as a source of blessing and strength to us in our growing process will continue to strengthen and bless us, as long as we need them. As we abide in a spirit of appreciation for all that we have had, all that we have been, and all that we have been through, we prepare ourself for the greater good that is even now coming our way. Remember when you first fell in love? It was probably sometime in your teens, and it was exciting, painful, wonderful, and terrifying. You probably thought that you had experienced the greatest thing in your life. Then, as you grew and matured, you came to know that loving is an ever-evolving experience. Life is also an ever-evolving experience. It never stands still; it never arrives at a point of sublime suspension. This is true also about wisdom and the knowing of wisdom.

Immaturity is plagued with the burden of not knowing that it doesn't know. Maturity is wondrously blessed with the realization that it does not know. Rejoice and give thanks that you don't know. Obviously we should not give thanks for ignorance, but rather we should rejoice in the awareness that even now there is a spirit of intelligence that is ready

122

to reveal itself to us. It is the spirit of freedom from resistance that is a keynote in our growing process.

In our human world of material and physical competitiveness, it has been impressed upon us over and over that to fight the good fight is noble. Even in Scriptures we are admonished to fight. "Acquit yourselves like men and fight." "Fight the good fight of the faith." By word and example, men have been led to believe that it is honorable to fight for God, for country, for family, for self, and for the things in this world that are desirable. Jesus, however, said; "You have heard that it was said, 'An eye for an eye and a tooth for a tooth.' But I say to you, Do not resist one who is evil. But if any one strikes you on the right cheek, turn to him the other also; and if any one would sue you and take away your coat, let him have your cloak as well; and if any one forces you to go one mile, go with him two miles. Give to him who begs from you, and do not refuse him who would borrow from you." The life and ministry of Jesus Christ was an exemplification of nonresistance.

To many people, the idea of nonresistance seems to smack of weakness, a lack of resolve. But it usually takes a great deal more in the way of resolve and courage and strength to be nonresistant than it does to fight. So long as man has existed in the consciousness of not knowing, he has developed elaborate rationales for fighting; on the physical level he has even developed bodily functions and organs that assist him in conflict. When man is confronted with fear, the instinct to fight or flee is basic. Adrenalin is pumped into the bloodstream, enabling man to reach to fantastic heights of prowess and energy. It was a good thing that man could fight; it was good that he had the capacity to rise to the occasion and thus protect himself by fleeing from or overcoming his foe. As we attain conscious Self-awareness, coming to know ourself to be God expressing Himself as us according to our consciousness of Him, we can see that we no longer need this instinct. We now have the realization that we do not have to fight. We don't have to fight God, we don't have to fight other men, we don't have to fight the elements, *we don't have to fight!* In our expanding consciousness of our unity with all that God is, we have the ability to meet any challenge that comes to us and to rise above it in nobility, in dignity, and with every expectation of being freed from its limitations.

You can, you know, be set free from any inharmony, any disease, any limitation in the world. In your unity with God, you do indeed have a majority! From this day forth you can manifest an ever greater degree of your heritage that is unity, and in that unity you can manifest the kingdom that was prepared for you from the beginning of time. Conscious Self-awareness is the genesis of the dominion and authority by which you shall return to the "garden" from whence you came. Have a happy journey in the knowledge that the glory that awaits you along the path will transcend any vision you have ever dreamed.